THURGOOD MARSHALL

ALSO BY JAMES HASKINS

The Day Martin Luther King, Jr., Was Shot
Rosa Parks: My Story, with Rosa Parks
The Life and Death of Martin Luther King, Jr.
The 60s Reader, with Kathleen Benson

THURGOOD MARSHALL

A Life for Justice

JAMES HASKINS

HENRY HOLT AND COMPANY | | NEW YORK

I am grateful to Kathy Benson,
Ann L. Kalkhoff, and
Kristin Straw for their help.

Copyright © 1992 by James Haskins
All rights reserved, including the right to reproduce
this book or portions thereof in any form.
First edition
Published by Henry Holt and Company, Inc.,
115 West 18th Street, New York, New York 10011.
Published simultaneously in Canada by Fitzhenry & Whiteside Ltd.,
91 Granton Drive, Richmond Hill, Ontario L4B 2N5.

Library of Congress Cataloging-in-Publication Data
Haskins, James.
Thurgood Marshall: a life for justice / Jim Haskins.
Includes bibliographical references and index.
Summary: Examines the life and accomplishments of the first black
judge to be appointed to the Supreme Court.
ISBN 0-8050-2095-0
1. Marshall, Thurgood, 1908—Juvenile literature.   2. Afro-
American judges—Biography—Juvenile literature.   [1. Marshall,
Thurgood, 1908–   . 2. Judges. 3. United States.   Supreme Court—
Biography. 4. Afro-Americans—Biography.] I. Title.
KF8745.M34H37 1992   347.73'2634—dc20
[B]   [347.3073534]   [B]   91-46251

Printed in the United States of America
on acid-free paper.∞

1   3   5   7   9   10   8   6   4   2

To Michael

Contents

THURGOOD MARSHALL

1

Goody

As an undergraduate in the 1920s, Thurgood Marshall attended Lincoln University, a small black college in Pennsylvania. The nearest town, Oxford, was mostly white, and the local people did not look kindly on the students from Lincoln. At the local movie theater, blacks could sit only in the balcony, never in the orchestra seats below. Everyone at Lincoln thought this was ridiculous, but no one had dared to challenge the rules of the movie house until Thurgood and a group of his friends decided to do so.

The ringleader was a student named John Little, but Thurgood talked many of his friends into helping out. They organized the desegregation of the Oxford movie theater. One night Little and Thurgood and four others set off for the movie theater. The six students purchased six tickets. The ticket seller said they would have to sit in the balcony. When they asked why, she told them it was the rule.

Before they even left the ticket window, the six students saw two more groups of Lincoln students approaching. Nervous but drawing comfort from the fact that they were not alone, Thurgood and his group entered the theater. It was only about one-third full and there were plenty of seats in the orchestra. Instead of climbing the stairs to the balcony, they marched down the aisle to the front and took seats. The other Lincoln students, who had come in after them, did the same. When the young white male usher told them they weren't supposed to sit there, they ignored him.

Seeing that the usher wasn't going to do anything further, one of the white men in the audience moved to a seat behind Thurgood and whispered, "Nigger, why don't you all just get out of here and go sit where you belong." Thurgood responded that he had paid for his ticket and would sit anywhere he pleased. After a few more angry exchanges in loud whispers, the man moved away. No one bothered the students for the rest of the movie, and from that time on, Lincoln students sat wherever they pleased at the Oxford movie theater.

While the students were delighted over their victory, they realized that the same tactics would not have worked in a town larger than Oxford. "We found out that they only had one fat cop in the whole town," Thurgood wrote to his father, "and they wouldn't have had the nerve or the room in the jail to arrest all of us. But the amazing thing was, when we were leaving we just walked out with all those other people and they didn't do anything, didn't say a thing, didn't even look at us—at least, as far as I know. I'm not sure I like being invisible, but maybe it's better than being put to shame and not able to respect yourself."

Thurgood Marshall did not know it at the time, but he would choose to devote most of the rest of his life to being one of the most highly visible fighters for the rights and self-respect of black people. He did not lead marches like Martin Luther King, Jr. Instead, he worked through the legal system, persuading the interpreters of the U.S. Constitution that the framework for modern-day equal rights existed in that document. Through the court decisions he won, he helped to lay the legal basis for full equality for black people.

Thurgood Marshall was born in Baltimore, Maryland, on July 2, 1908. His parents were William Canfield Marshall and Norma Williams Marshall, and Thurgood was their second son. His brother, Aubrey, was three years older. Thurgood was a chubby little boy with curly hair and dark eyes. Friends and family remarked at what a beautiful child he was and that he would grow up to be a handsome man.

When Thurgood was born, his parents decided to name him after his paternal grandfather because they were very proud of the older man. A rough and tough sailor, he had gone by just one name, Marshall. When the Union North and the Confederate South went to war over slavery in the 1860s, Marshall wanted to join the Union Army to fight on the side of the North. But when he tried to sign up, he was told that he needed to have two names. Marshall couldn't decide on the first name Thoroughgood or Thornygood, so he signed up under both. Somehow, in the records of the Union Army, he became two different men, and after the war was over and Thoroughgood/Thornygood Marshall was old enough to collect an army pension, he was able to collect two. He collected one pension as Thoroughgood Marshall and the other pension as Thornygood Marshall.

William and Norma Marshall laughed about all that, and when their second son was born, they decided to put both his grandfather's names on his birth certificate. So, Thurgood Marshall's birth certificate has two names. From the beginning, the family favored Thoroughgood, because calling the little boy two names would have been confusing. But more often than not, they just called the little boy by the nickname Goody.

When he was old enough to choose, the little boy decided he liked Thoroughgood better. But he didn't much like spelling it. By the time he was seven and in second grade, he had shortened the name to Thurgood, and that is how he has been known ever since.

There were odd names on Mrs. Marshall's side of the family, too. One of the grandfathers had been named Isaiah O. B. Williams. The initials, he said, stood for Olive Branch. In the Bible, an olive branch stands for peace. He, too, was a sailor, and he traveled to many ports before settling down in Baltimore to open a grocery store on Denmeade Street. He got married and had six children. All received special names after the things and places their father loved. His first daughter was Avonia Delicia and his first son was Avon, both named after the Avon River, by which the famous English writer William Shakespeare had lived. The next daughter was named Denmedia Marketa, after the store. Another, Thurgood's mother, was named Norma Arica. *Norma* was a tragic opera, and Arica was the port in Chile where Isaiah had first heard it. Two other children were named Fearless Mentor and Ravine Silestria. No one can figure out where those names came from. Norma Marshall, her husband, and their sons enjoyed the sound of those strange names.

They were very proud of their ancestors. Thurgood's great-grandfather was an African slave who had been brought to the United States from the Belgian Congo, which is now an independent country called Zaire. As an adult, Thurgood loved to repeat the story told to him by his parents:

Way back before the Civil War, this rich man from Maryland went to the Congo on a hunting expedition or something. The whole time he was there, this little black boy trailed him around. So when they got ready to come back to this country, they just picked him up and brought him along. The years passed and he grew up, and boy, he grew into one mean man. One day his owner came to him and said, 'You're so evil I got to get rid of you. But I haven't the heart to sell you or give you to another man. So I'll tell you what I'll do: if you'll get out of the town, county, and state, I'll give you your freedom.' Well, my great-grandfather never said a word, just looked at him. And he walked off the place, settled a couple miles away, raised his family and lived there until he died. And nobody ever laid a hand on him.

It was this man's son, Thurgood's grandfather Thoroughgood or Thornygood Marshall, who had later volunteered to serve in the Union Army.

William Marshall was a waiter on the Baltimore & Ohio (B&O) Railroad. Norma Marshall was a schoolteacher. Not long after Thurgood was born, the Marshalls moved to Harlem in New York City, where Thurgood spent his first five years.

Harlem was quite far away from the main section of the city and had been farmland for many years. By the late 1800s it had become a suburb of the city. Then, plans were made to build an elevated subway line that would connect Harlem to downtown Manhattan.

As soon as construction on the subway began, white real estate developers started to build apartment buildings in Harlem. Many buildings went up. In fact, work on those buildings went far quicker than work on the subway line. Suddenly, the developers had a whole bunch of empty buildings and no subway. They were liable for mortgage payments and had to rent to someone. Some of them started renting to black people, often at higher rents than they would have charged whites. The white people who already lived in Harlem did not want black neighbors. In many areas, blacks were not allowed to live. The Marshalls, who lived at 140th Street and Lenox Avenue, remembered seeing signs that said, "This part of 135th Street guaranteed against Negro invasion."

There were Harlem restaurants and theaters that would not admit blacks. In theaters that did allow them in, they had to sit in the balcony. But the older Marshalls knew that conditions for black people in Harlem were better than they were in Baltimore, where racial segregation was much more strict and where black people had very few rights. Thurgood was too young to be aware of how black people were treated when the family lived in Harlem. Most of his early memories recall the time after the family moved back to Baltimore.

That was in 1913, when Thurgood was five. William Marshall left the railroad and got a job as a steward in the restaurant of the Gibson Island Club, a country club in Baltimore that did not admit blacks or Jews as members. Norma Marshall got work teaching at a local public school. The move seems to have affected Thurgood, for his personality changed about that time. His aunt Denmedia recalled that when he was very young he was timid. "But one day—he must have been around five—he stopped crying and became a pretty tough guy. Now, I don't know what caused the change. Maybe the boys slapped his head."

Perhaps it was neighborhood boys or the other men in his family who brought about the change, but a tough Goody was far happier than a timid Goody would have been in the Marshall family. William Marshall loved to argue. If he'd had the opportunity, he would like to have been a lawyer. In his free time, he often would go to the local courthouse to sit in the courtroom and watch cases being tried. At home he acted like a lawyer, demanding that his sons back up whatever they said with reasonable arguments. As his sons grew older, they got better at arguing in this way, and they loved nothing better than to have loud discussions around the dinner table. Neighbors of the Marshalls on Druid Hill Avenue used to complain about the arguing and shouting, but after a while they got used to it.

Aubrey and Thurgood didn't always confine their disputes to arguing. Sometimes, they got into fights. Both were strong willed and determined to stand up for themselves. The trouble for Thurgood was that Aubrey was three years older than he was. One time, when Aubrey was thirteen and Thurgood was ten, they were carrying a wagonload of groceries home from the market. The wagon tipped over, and each boy blamed the other. First, they yelled at each other, then they started punching. The fight was over very quickly because the older and stronger Aubrey beat up Thurgood. For Thurgood, it was a lesson learned. He decided it was best to win by arguing and that he would not try to use physical force, at least not where his brother was concerned. The two brothers had very different personalities. "We lived on a respectable street," Thurgood recalled, "but behind us there were back alleys where the roughnecks and the tough kids hung out. When it was time for dinner, my mother used to go to the front door and call my older brother. Then she'd go to the *back* door and call me."

With both parents working at steady jobs, the Marshalls were better off than most other black people in Baltimore. They had a comfortable home, never went hungry, and always had enough clothing, although young Thurgood mostly wore hand-me-downs from Aubrey. William Marshall enjoyed spending time with his sons. One of their favorite pastimes was going down to the railroad depot to watch the B&O Railroad trains. Their father would tell stories of his years working as a steward in dining cars on the B&O. He particularly admired the design of the trains and told his sons exactly how they worked. Thurgood developed a lifelong interest in trains as a result of these outings with his father.

As soon as they were old enough, both boys worked part-time jobs. The family did not need the money, but the elder Marshalls agreed that their sons should understand the importance of work and the value of money. When he was very young, Thurgood ran errands for neighbors. Later, he shined shoes. By the time he was an adolescent, he was working as a delivery boy for a hatmaker named Mr. Schoen, who ran Schoen's Specialty Shop.

While delivering a load of hats one day, he had his first serious encounter with racism. He was carrying a stack of hat boxes so high that he couldn't see in front of him. He had to take the trolley, and when it arrived, he started to step up. Suddenly, someone grabbed his arm, and he heard a man say, "Nigger, don't you never push in front of no white lady again." Thurgood dropped the boxes as he came down backward off the step. He whirled around and punched the small white man who had grabbed his arm. The man punched him back, and the two were still fighting when a policeman arrived to break it up.

Luckily for Thurgood, he knew the policeman, whose name was Army Matthews. Black people in Baltimore liked Army. Although he was a white man, just like every other policeman in Baltimore, he treated black people like human beings and was fair to them. He was willing to listen to Thurgood's side of the

story. Most other policemen in Baltimore would simply have arrested any black youth who had struck a
white man, no matter what the reason.

Army Matthews listened to Thurgood, and then he
listened to the white man. He did not know whom to
believe. So, he arrested both of them. Young Thurgood was thinking about how much trouble he was
in. He was being arrested for the first time in his life,
and he was sure he would lose his job with Schoen's
Specialty Shop. Then, in walked Mr. Schoen himself.
Not only did Mr. Schoen pay his fine, but he also
assured Thurgood that he was still an employee in
good standing.

When Thurgood got home and told his mother and
Aubrey what had happened, Aubrey called him a fool
for hitting a white man. Thurgood knew he had taken
a big chance doing that. If Army Marshall hadn't come
on the scene, he would have been arrested and the
white man would have been let go. Blacks weren't
even supposed to look white people straight in the
eye, much less push in front of them onto a trolley car
or hit them. But Thurgood also believed that he had
been right to defend himself against the white man
who had grabbed him and called him "Nigger." And
he knew his father would agree.

William Marshall was a proud man. He wanted his
sons to be proud, too. As soon as they were old enough
to understand, he told them, "If anybody calls you
Nigger, you not only got my permission to fight him—
you got my orders."

But there were indignities to growing up black in a southern city in the early years of this century that Thurgood could not fight because they were too all-pervasive. The entire legal structure was built on seg-regating the races, keeping them apart, and treating black people as second-class citizens. Separate places to sit on street cars, separate water fountains and restrooms, different rules for blacks and whites—all these made life difficult for black people. In 1988, eighty-year-old Thurgood remembered another time when he was downtown: "I remember when I was a teenager in Baltimore there were no restroom facili-ties downtown for Negroes. I had 'an urge,' and I started thinking where to go, but there was no place to go. So I jumped on the trolley car and went home. I got off at my stop and had the key in the door, and then right there in the middle of the afternoon right on the steps, it all went. . . . Now, that's a little more than inconvenience. And guess what, I remember it."

The Marshall boys did not have racial troubles at school because they attended all-black schools. The Baltimore public school system was segregated in those days; white children went to white schools, black children to black schools. Teachers were segre-gated, too, and so Mrs. Marshall taught at the same elementary school that her sons attended.

Of the two, Aubrey was the better student. He would take time to study and do his homework. Thur-good could not be bothered with studying, and he was smart enough so that he could get by anyway. To him, there were so many other things to think about that school subjects were not all that important.

He had a reputation as a cutup in class. Students who acted up were punished by being sent to the basement, where they had to spend hours memorizing the Constitution. Thurgood didn't pay much attention to what he was memorizing and wouldn't have understood a lot of it even if he had paid attention, but some of it sank in. He wondered why there was no direct mention of slavery or black people in the original Constitution. Slaves were referred to only as "other persons." Slavery and blacks were mentioned only in the amendments to the Constitution. He also wondered why there were so many amendments to the Constitution about equal rights, when he knew very well that black people did not enjoy equal rights in America.

When Thurgood took these questions to his father, William Marshall explained that when the Constitution was being written back in 1787, the former colonies could not agree on the question of slavery. So, they compromised by not mentioning it at all. They didn't even discuss seriously the idea of including women, Native Americans, or white men who did not own property in their definition of citizens. Back then, only white male property owners were considered citizens.

Slavery and other issues continued to divide northern and southern states for nearly seventy-five years, until at last the South seceded from the Union and formed the Confederate States of America. The North, which wanted to keep the Union intact, went to war against the Confederacy. After the North won, the Thirteenth, Fourteenth, and Fifteenth amendments to the Constitution were adopted. The Thirteenth (1865) outlawed slavery. The Fourteenth (1868) guaranteed that all Americans were equal citizens. The Fifteenth (1870) guaranteed all adult male citizens the right to vote. For a little more than ten years, while federal troops occupied the South, blacks there did enjoy the right to vote and other rights of citizenship. But after the inauguration of President Rutherford B. Hayes in 1877, federal troops were pulled out of the southern states. White people across the nation were calling for unity between the North and the South so that the nation could industrialize and prosper. They were no longer interested in black rights, and they quickly moved to make blacks second-class citizens. They did so by passing laws that came to be called Jim Crow laws, after a minstrel character patterned on an old black man who did a funny dance. But there was nothing funny about laws denying blacks their equal rights as citizens.

Blacks did not willingly agree to these laws. In fact, they fought them. But white southerners formed secret organizations such as the Ku Klux Klan to frighten blacks into submission by lynchings, the killing of blacks by mobs of whites. Those blacks who tried to take their grievances to court found that whites were no longer interested in black rights. In 1896 the United

States Supreme Court ruled in the case of *Plessy v. Ferguson*, the *v.* being short for *versus*, or against. It was the opinion of the court that segregation on public transportation was legal as long as equal facilities were provided for both races. Blacks never did enjoy equal facilities. What was provided for them was separate but not equal.

Separate public restrooms were provided for white men and women. Both women and men had to share the restrooms for "colored." City public libraries had numerous branches for whites, but only one, if any, for "colored." On public buses, front rows were reserved for whites. Blacks could sit in the back rows unless the rows for whites were filled and whites were left standing. In that event, blacks had to give up their seats to whites. Also, blacks had to pay at the front door of the bus but then go around to the side door to board.

Black schools were not as well equipped as white schools. Textbooks and gym equipment in black schools were castoffs from white schools. Black schoolteachers were paid less than white schoolteachers. School buses were provided for white students. Black students had to walk to school.

William Marshall told his younger son that what was in the Constitution and its amendments was the way things were supposed to be, not the way they actually were. Someday, he said, that would change, and things would be the way the Constitution said they should be. While the elder Marshall was not happy about the reason Thurgood was reading so much of the Constitution, he was pleased that his younger son was reading it, for it is the document on which all United States laws are based. As Thurgood grew older, his father would sometimes take him to the courthouse to watch a trial. He would point out when a lawyer was making a good argument or why he thought a legal argument could be made better. And always, at home, in discussions around the dinner table, William Marshall would insist that his sons give logical reasons for their statements, just as if they were in a court of law.

William Marshall never said what he wanted his sons to be when they grew up. Secretly, he might have wished that at least one of them could become a lawyer. But he knew that it was very hard to be a black lawyer. The whole legal system was run by whites. Most blacks in the system were defendants. There were very few black lawyers because most of the time when a black lawyer went to court, he was almost assured of losing his case. Juries were always made up of whites, and they would not believe a black lawyer. Only if he had a white lawyer helping him could he have any hope of victory for his client.

Norma Marshall, on the other hand, had very definite plans for her sons' careers. She wanted Aubrey, the better student, to be a doctor and Thurgood to be a dentist. Next to ministers, black doctors were the most highly respected men in the black community.

They made a very good living treating patients. Black dentists also made a good living and enjoyed respect in the community. They couldn't charge as much as doctors, but they had more and steadier work than black doctors. Some white doctors would treat black patients, and many black people preferred to go to white doctors than to black doctors because they thought the white doctors were better. There were few white dentists who would treat blacks.

Thurgood's grandmother, who lived with the family, thought the boys should know how to cook and did her best to teach them. She often said that a black cook never lacked for a job. Thurgood enjoyed learning how to cook, and the skill served him well in later years. His specialities were crab soup and chocolate cake.

Both Aubrey and Thurgood attended Douglass High School in Baltimore. It was an all-black high school named after Frederick Douglass, a famous black leader who had lived in the 1800s. Born into slavery, he had escaped to the North, educated himself, and become a powerful spokesman for the cause of abolition, the ending of slavery. All the students at Douglass High studied the life of Frederick Douglass and were taught to be proud of the role he had played in bringing about the end of slavery. Support for the abolitionist cause in the North had led to the Civil War, for the southern slave states had seceded from the Union and formed the Confederate States of

America rather than allow slavery to be outlawed. The North had fought to keep the Union of the states, and in winning the war also won the end of slavery.

At Douglass High, Thurgood played football and joined clubs. A handsome young man, he had no trouble getting dates. He loved high school and managed to get good grades without doing much studying. Following in Aubrey's footsteps, he got summer jobs working the New York–to–Washington run on the B&O Railroad. The first summer he worked on the railroad, he was given a uniform with pants that were too short. Thurgood was growing, and rapidly on the way to his full height of six feet, two inches. He felt silly in too-short pants and complained to the chief steward. "Boy," said the steward, "we can get a man to fit the pants a lot easier than we can get the pants to fit the man. Why don't you just kinda scroonch down in 'em a little more?" Thurgood scroonched.

Aubrey graduated from Douglass High and went off to Lincoln University, and Thurgood enjoyed being the only Marshall at Douglass High. Teachers and other students naturally compared the brothers, which was hard for both boys. Thurgood was more outgoing by nature and had always been popular. He appreciated not having to compare grades with Aubrey any more.

Aubrey enjoyed college. When he came home, which was often because Lincoln was not that far away, he was full of new ideas and eager to argue them at the family dinner table. He talked about Lincoln so much that Thurgood came to feel that he knew Lincoln too well to go to college there. He also wasn't sure he wanted to go to the same college as Aubrey because people so often compared them. Besides, it had occurred to him that he didn't have to go to an all-black college. There were schools in the North that would accept black students.

He brought up the idea of going to another school to his father. Perhaps he could get a football scholarship to a white college in the North. But his father thought he would have a difficult time at a predominantly white school. After all, being admitted didn't mean he would be accepted. He would have to live separate from the white students. There would be very few other black students. He might be lonely, and he would be so far from home that he would not be able to see his family often. His father advised that he would be much better off at a small black college like Lincoln, and by his senior year Thurgood realized that he would probably be following his brother. His mother pawned her diamond engagement ring to pay his tuition. She was unable to raise the necessary money to get it back before it was sold.

Thus, Thurgood Marshall ended his childhood years knowing how important his education was to his parents. He prepared to go away from home for the first time already aware that the larger world was not a very friendly place for blacks. But his parents had instilled in him a strong sense of himself, and he left home for college firmly believing that with his intelligence and his personality he could be just about anything he wanted to be.

2

Nogood and Iron Shoes

L incoln University is located in Chester County in the Pennsylvania countryside near the small town of Oxford, forty miles from Philadelphia. Founded after the Civil War to educate the children of slaves, it began with an all-white faculty and an all-black student body. By the middle 1920s, when Aubrey and Thurgood Marshall attended, the student body had changed. It was still all black, but the students were mostly the children of middle-class black people. Three things had not changed. The student body was small (about three hundred altogether). The students were all male, and the faculty was all white.

One of the students at Lincoln while Thurgood was there was Langston Hughes, the great black writer and poet. He enrolled at Christmastime 1925 as a twenty-three-year-old freshman and was in the same class as Thurgood. Another student was Benjamin Nnamdi Azikiwe, a young man from Africa. Many years later, he would become the first president of Nigeria. Lincoln was the first American college to educate African students, and another was Kwame Nkrumah, who would become the first prime minister and president of Ghana. Cab Calloway, later a great entertainer and band leader, was a friend of Thurgood's at Lincoln.

If Thurgood Marshall had enjoyed high school, he loved college even more. He wasted no time making friends, and he enjoyed going to parties, playing cards, and taking the train to Philadelphia. There he found a substantial black population and lots of clubs and restaurants and theaters for blacks. Langston Hughes later wrote, "Rough and ready, loud and wrong, good-natured and uncouth—these are phrases some of Lincoln classmates still use to describe the raucous undergraduate."

In their sophomore year, Hughes and Thurgood enjoyed tormenting the freshmen. The practice of "hazing" was a tradition. Sophomores humiliated the freshmen every chance they got—insisting the younger students call them "Sir" and wait on them hand and foot. They made freshmen wear strange outfits. Apparently that particular sophomore class was so hard on the freshmen that the freshmen revolted. In retaliation, some twenty-six sophomores lay in wait one night and shaved the heads of almost the entire freshman class. In response, the administration threatened to expel the sophomores involved, including Thurgood. The sophomore class, however, appointed Langston Hughes to draw up a statement pleading collective guilt, and the administration relented and let Thurgood and the others stay at Lincoln.

Undaunted, Thurgood continued to devote much of his energy to making life difficult for the school administration. A favorite pastime among the students was calling strikes against the school, especially over the food and the rules. There was often an "edge" to the strikes because they were the only way the students could get back at the all-white faculty, whom they felt didn't care about them. But mostly, the strikes were in fun. "You had to be careful of timing," Thurgood told Ponchitta Pierce of *Ebony* magazine in 1965. "You couldn't strike in the beginning of the year because there was a backlog of applicants to replace you and you couldn't act up at the end of the year because of marks." He put a sign on his dormitory room that read "Land of the Disinherited." He stayed up all night playing cards and became an expert at pinochle.

Bored with his course work, Thurgood spent more time reading library books that were not assigned than reading the works required by his teachers. Still, he was smart enough to keep his grades up with minimal studying. In the meantime, as in high school, he worked part-time. During the school year he worked as a grocery clerk and baker. In the summers, he returned to the B&O Railroad as a dining car waiter.

One thing he enjoyed greatly was participating in bull sessions in the dormitory, where he lived with other male students. The young men loved to argue about everything, and Thurgood found that his father had trained him well to back up his statements with logic. He was so good that he joined the school debating club, where he soon became a star. Other students called him Wrathful Marshall because he could out-debate his opponents so well that they felt whipped at the end of a contest. It was the debating team, more than his regular courses, that led him to read so many books; he was gathering facts for the arguments he presented in debate.

Thurgood realized that he could be very persuasive, and one October he decided to see what he could do to improve school spirit. The football team had a dismal record and hadn't won or tied a game all season. So Thurgood got up at a pregame pep rally and made a twenty-minute speech about how the team could win if the students were behind it. At the game, the students cheered as if their team were the champions. While the Lincoln team didn't win, it managed a tie.

Thurgood formed the Weekend Club, an unofficial group whose members would not be caught dead on campus on the weekend unless one of the athletic teams had a game. Thurgood spent most of his weekends in Philadelphia. The main reason was Vivien Burey, whom everyone called Buster, a student at the University of Pennsylvania with whom he had fallen in love. They were the same age and in the same year at college. It did not take them long to realize that they shared the same interests. Thurgood made the forty-mile trip to see Buster so often that he decided it made more sense to just get married.

His parents weren't sure that marriage was such a good idea. His mother, especially, didn't feel that he was mature enough to take on the responsibilities of married life. But Thurgood, using his debating skills, argued that he loved Buster and was ready for marriage. Buster also succeeded in convincing her parents that she would be happiest if she quit the University of Pennsylvania and married Thurgood. The wedding took place in the summer after their junior year of college, when both were just twenty years old.

Thurgood's senior year at Lincoln was much different from the previous three years. Instead of living in a dormitory with other male students, he lived with Buster in a small apartment in Oxford. While he still enjoyed debating and spending time at the library gathering "ammunition" for his arguments, he much preferred to spend his free time with her. Buster, who had worked part-time as a secretary while attending the University of Pennsylvania, got a job as a secretary in Oxford. Thurgood was determined that his wife's working was just temporary and looked forward to the time when he could get a job and support her.

Thurgood had majored in predentistry while at Lincoln. The next step was dentistry school. But as his senior year wore on, he realized that he just wasn't interested in being a dentist. What he really wanted was to study law.

When he confided his thoughts to Buster, she told him she thought he'd look better in a suit and tie than in a dentist's white coat. His mother was disappointed that he would not become a dentist, but she knew better than to try to influence her son, who knew his own mind. She had to be content that at least Aubrey was following the path she had hoped and was in his third year of medical school. Thurgood's father was delighted.

In order to afford law school tuition, Thurgood and Buster had to move in with the Marshalls. Thurgood would have preferred to attend the nearby University of Maryland. But Maryland did not accept black students, and there was no black law school in the state. The idea that he did not have the same choices as whites rankled Thurgood. Indeed, he never completely got over his anger at the unfairness of the racial segregation system. The thought crossed Thurgood's mind that perhaps it was time that a black student tried to integrate the University of Maryland, but he never seriously considered being that student. After all, the university was not the Oxford, Pennsylvania, movie house. Maryland, being a state university, could call on state troopers and the best lawyers in the state to prevent integration. So, Thurgood Marshall applied to the closest black law school, the one at Howard University in Washington, D.C.

In 1930, Thurgood graduated from Lincoln University *cum laude*, which means "with honors." While he waited to hear if he had been accepted, Thurgood got a job selling insurance. He was relieved when one week later he got his acceptance from Howard. It took only a few days for him to decide that he was not cut out for sales work, no matter how good his skills at arguing might be. Part of him wondered if it wasn't too much of a luxury to try to attend law school at that particular time. After all, the country was in a deep economic depression, which had started after the crash of the Stock Market in New York in the fall of 1929. In the years following, it would be referred to as the Great Depression. Many people lost their jobs and money was tight for just about everyone. Sometimes, Thurgood thought about how he could help his family more by getting a job and helping with expenses. But he was excited about going to law school, and he convinced himself that once he had his law degree he would be able to make more money for his family.

By this time, he and Buster had moved into the Marshall home on Druid Hill Avenue and into the room that had been Thurgood's ever since he was a small child. Buster found a job as a secretary in Baltimore. Once school began, Thurgood began commuting to Washington, D.C., getting up before dawn each weekday morning to take the train to the nation's capital. In the early afternoon, he took the train back to Baltimore, arriving in time for his afternoon job. In the evening, after dinner with his family, he would study until midnight.

For the first time in his life, Thurgood really enjoyed studying for his courses. He found that he loved to read the law and to contribute to class discussion. By the end of his first year—in spite of his grueling schedule of commuting, working part-time, and studying— he was first in his class. But the hard work paid off. His position as first in his class made him eligible for a job at the Howard University Law School library. Now his job and his studies were in the same place, which made life a lot easier.

Thurgood entered Howard University Law School when that institution was going through great changes. Until the late 1920s, the law school had reflected the position of black lawyers in the United States. *Negro Professional Men*, a survey done in the early 1930s by the black historian Carter G. Woodson, revealed that there were few black lawyers in the South and that those few were not highly regarded as leaders in the black community. Most of them were without partners and had to devote themselves to small cases that would earn fees. They did not have the time or the means to serve the community.

Accordingly, the few black law schools did not spend much time teaching their students more than basic law. They had no vision about how the law could be made to work for the black community. In 1929, Howard University Law School had an enroll-

ment of more than eighty, many of them part-time
students taking night courses and working at regular
jobs during the day. Most of the teachers were white
and only part-time instructors. The school had a lousy
reputation.

Mordecai Johnson was president of Howard University at the time. He later said that none other than
U.S. Supreme Court Justice Louis Brandeis had advised him to make reorganization of the law school a
top priority: "He told me that the one thing I could
do was to build a law school and train men to get
the constitutional rights of our people. He said the
Supreme Court knew the rights for Negro equality
were in the Constitution but that no lawyer, Negro or
white, was skilled enough to get them out. He said,
'Once you train lawyers to do this, the Supreme Court
will have to hand your people their civil and constitutional rights.' "

Johnson immediately set about making Howard
University Law School the "West Point of Negro leadership," by which he meant the most rigorous training
ground for the attorneys who would lead black people
in the fight for their rights. He hired Charles Hamilton
Houston as the new vice dean of Howard University
Law School.

Houston was born in 1895, the year before the
U.S. Supreme Court decided in the case of *Plessy v.
Ferguson* that segregation was constitutional as long
as equal facilities were provided for blacks. Both his
parents had jobs, and his father earned a law degree

by attending evening classes at Howard University
Law School, later setting up a successful law practice
serving middle-class blacks in Washington, D.C.
Houston attended M Street High School, one of the
finest all-black schools in the country. He graduated
at age sixteen and was the only black student in the
class of 1915 at Amherst College in Massachusetts,
where he was elected to Phi Beta Kappa, the academic
honor society. He graduated with honors and then
taught English at Howard University. When the
United States entered World War I, Houston and other
Howard faculty persuaded the federal government to
establish a black officer's training camp. Houston attended that camp in Des Moines, Iowa, and later
served as an officer with the army in France.

After the war ended, returning black soldiers believed they had earned some rights in return for
fighting for their country. But whites didn't see it that
way. Back in Washington, D.C., Houston witnessed
several "race riots," which in those days meant
whites beating up blacks, sparked by incidents of
blacks not remembering "their place" as second-class
citizens. He decided to dedicate himself to the cause
of black people's rights and enrolled at Harvard University Law School in Massachusetts, the best law
school in the country. He earned his law degree there
in 1922 and his doctoral degree a year later. He was
the first black elected to the editorial board of the
Harvard Law Review.

In 1924, Houston joined his father's law firm and

also returned to teaching at Howard University Law School. Three years later, he helped conduct the survey on black lawyers in the United States on which Carter G. Woodson later based his survey of black professional men in America. When Mordecai Johnson hired him as vice dean of the Howard University Law School in 1929, Houston saw his chance to work for his belief that the Constitution could be made to work for black people. The profession needed a core of bright, energetic, young black lawyers to attack unfair national, state, and local laws in the courts. He set out to make Howard University Law School a training ground for young black lawyers who would devote their energies to really helping the black community.

Houston quickly went about reducing the enrollment at Howard University Law School, and by 1933, there were thirty-seven students, down from over eighty in 1929. In 1931 he started hiring black teachers and full-time teachers. By 1933 Howard had four full-time faculty, three of whom were black, and seven part-time faculty, four of whom were black.

In addition to heading the law school, Charles Houston also taught courses: most importantly, a series of civil rights seminars on how existing laws could be made to work for black people. In his sophomore year, Thurgood took a course in civil rights law with Houston, the first time such a course had ever been taught. Thurgood found Houston to be a hard taskmaster. "First off, you thought he was a mean so-and-so," he recalled in the 1980s.

He used to tell us that doctors could bury their mistakes, but lawyers couldn't. And he'd drive home to us that we would be competing not only with white lawyers but with really well-trained white lawyers, so there just wasn't any point in crying in our beer about being Negroes. . . . He was so tough we used to call him "Iron Shoes" and "Cement Pants." . . . But he was a sweet man once you saw what he was up to. He was absolutely fair, and the door to his office was always open. He made it clear to all of us that when we were done, we were expected to go out and do something with our lives.

In Charles Hamilton Houston's civil rights seminar, Thurgood began to see that the passages about equal opportunity that he had memorized from the Constitution back in Baltimore could be used to gain more rights for black people. The key to opening doors for black Americans was contained in the very law of the nation. Through the efforts of Houston and the lawyers he groomed to follow in his footsteps, the bulletin of Howard University Law School could proudly state within a decade that all the faculty members were active in the struggle for equality of opportunity and through their courses prepared students to carry on the battle. "No law school except Howard has a course devoted solely to ways and means of protecting and enlarging the liberties of its constituency," declared the bulletin. "Not only has Howard developed such a course—Civil Rights—but whenever possible it relates its regular law courses to the Negro—how can the accepted devices of the law be adapted to peculiar Negro problems?"

Thurgood learned that civil rights are rights of personal liberty that are guaranteed by the Thirteenth and Fourteenth amendments to the Constitution. He already knew from his high-school reading of the Constitution that these amendments had been passed by Congress and ratified, or agreed to, by the states after the Civil War, and that they had finally put mentions of slavery into the Constitution. The Thirteenth Amendment had abolished slavery. The Fourteenth Amendment had promised to all American citizens the "equal protection" of the law. But Thurgood had known even then that black people did not actually enjoy protection under the law. Especially in the South, black Americans were more often victimized by the law than protected by it. Southern states had laws that prevented blacks from eating in the same restaurants as whites, drinking from the same water fountains, riding in the same bus seats. In most cases, those state laws were counter to the federal laws and to the Thirteenth and Fourteenth amendments to the Constitution, the highest law of the land. Houston believed that it was possible to show that the Constitution and especially its Thirteenth and Fourteenth amendments were not being followed. And he instilled in Thurgood and his other students an excitement and hope that they might be able to help in that legal struggle.

Another professor who influenced Thurgood was William Hastie. Hastie was a cousin of Charles Hamilton Houston and a 1930 honor graduate of Harvard University Law School. Thurgood took a course in writing briefs with Hastie. In law, briefs are written summaries of all arguments on one side of a court case. The term *briefcase* describes the satchel in which lawyers carry their briefs. These written summaries are very important because judges often read briefs in order to decide whether a case should come before a court. In Hastie's class, Thurgood not only learned about briefs from listening, he also got practical experience.

The young and energetic black faculty at Howard University Law School didn't spend all their time teaching in the classroom. They were also putting into practice their ideas to help black people. Getting their students to help them with their outside cases not only benefited them—the students worked for free—but also benefited the students by giving them practical experience.

The case Thurgood worked on involved a young black college graduate named Thomas Hocutt, who had been refused admittance to the University of North Carolina School of Pharmacy. There was no pharmacy school for blacks in the state, and Hocutt believed that he should be admitted to the university pharmacy school. He felt that he had a case because back in 1896, some thirty-five years earlier, the United States Supreme Court had ruled that as long as a state provided "separate but equal facilities" for black people, it was not going against the Constitution. The 1896 case was *Plessy v. Ferguson*. Plessy was Homer Plessy, a New Orleans man who was seven-eighths white and one-eighth black. In 1890 he attempted to board the white section of a train going from New Orleans to Covington, Louisiana. The conductor refused him and told him to go to the "colored section." When the state of Louisiana began to try him for violating the segregation law, Plessy sought a ruling that would prevent the trial judge, John H. Ferguson, from proceeding with the trial. Plessy argued that the segregation law violated his constitutional rights. He believed that the Louisiana law violated the Fourteenth Amendment, which stated that no state "shall deny . . . the equal protection of the laws." Plessy lost his case in the Louisiana state courts and in the federal district courts to which he appealed. He then took his case all the way to the U.S. Supreme Court. Justice Henry Brown, who wrote the opinion for the Court, made a distinction between political equality, which was guaranteed by the Fourteenth Amendment, and social equality, which he said could not be guaranteed by law. As long as laws like Louisiana's were "enacted in good faith for the promotion of the public good, and not for the annoyance or oppression of a particular class," they were constitutional.

Homer Plessy and others who were opposed to segregation knew perfectly well that such laws did indeed oppress black people. But at the time, the nine justices of the U.S. Supreme Court were mostly men who believed in upholding segregation. One who disagreed was Justice John Marshall Harlan. But on the U.S. Supreme Court, the majority rules. The Court's ruling in *Plessy v. Ferguson* sealed the fate of blacks in the South for nearly sixty years.

While the Court's decision did not actually use the phrase "separate but equal" and did not state in so many words that segregation was constitutional, it wasn't long before many states in the South had decided that this was exactly what the Court meant. It was in the late 1890s and early 1900s that the most severe laws to separate the races were passed in the South. Eventually, they touched on every aspect of life, from mandating separate "white" and "colored" water fountains, to denying blacks and whites the right to play checkers together (Birmingham, Alabama) to forbidding black and white cotton mill workers to look out the same windows (South Carolina).

Thomas Hocutt, the black North Carolina student of pharmacy, would have liked to challenge the whole system of segregation, but he knew he would get nowhere. So, he decided to press his case on the basis of the separate but equal idea. The student knew very well that North Carolina had no separate but equal place for him to study pharmacy.

To help Professor Hastie prepare a brief on behalf of the North Carolina student, Thurgood went to the library and read everything he could on the Thirteenth and Fourteenth amendments to the Constitution and on the *Plessy v. Ferguson* case. With Hastie and other students in the class, he studied the statistics they had gathered on education expenditures by the state of North Carolina—the amount of money spent on black and white schools, the salaries paid to black and white teachers, the kinds of courses offered by the schools for both races. They were not suprised to find out that the state spent much more on educating its white students than it did on educating its blacks.

Thurgood took all this evidence and, using his best debating skills, wrote a brief for Professor Hastie that was remarkable for its logic. More than twenty years later, in 1957, Hastie, who by that time was a federal circuit court judge in Philadelphia, said that he had kept the brief: "Now and then," he said, "I take it out and look at it again, and I still admire it."

When it came time for Professor Hastie to go to North Carolina to argue the student's case in court, all the students at Howard were certain that he could prove that the state provided no separate but equal pharmacy school for black students. But simply proving that did not mean the student won his case. In fact, he lost.

The lawyer for the University of North Carolina argued that the school was not run by the government. Because students paid tuition, the school was a private institution. Therefore, it was not bound by the Fourteenth Amendment and its equal protection clause. The judge ruled in favor of the University, even though it was a state institution.

While Thurgood and the other students were upset over the unfairness of the verdict, Dean Houston and Professor Hastie were not. The decision would be appealed to a higher court. Even if it were lost on appeal, they had still made progress. After all, black people had not seriously challenged state laws in many years. Over time, the logic of their arguments would begin to settle into the minds of open-minded judges. Over time, they would have small victories, and eventually they would topple the whole notion of segregation. It might take many years, but they would do it.

Under Charles Hamilton Houston, Howard University Law School students learned much more than law. They learned how to remain optimistic in the face of defeat. They also learned that if they hoped to bring about change, they were going to have to put up with a great deal of hatred, not to mention physical danger. While there was segregation and discrimination in the North, the worst conditions for black people were in the South. There the main battle had to take place, and they would find themselves fighting for black rights in a hostile environment.

Houston also attempted to give his students practical experience arguing cases in court, because black lawyers did not have much of a history of being in court without white cocounsel. He started a system at Howard in which students and faculty played the roles of judge, jury, and opposing attorneys. They challenged the student attorney pleading his case at every opportunity, and any student who could win his case had to be good.

Thurgood Marshall thrived under this system and at Howard. He made many friends during his time there, for in spite of his fierce devotion to the study of law, he was an easy-going, joke-cracking, thoroughly likable fellow who earned many fond nicknames such as Nogood and Turkie. In 1933 he graduated from Howard University Law School at the top of his class and *magna cum laude*, which means with high honors. He had the right to the letters LL.B. after his name, letters that stand for Bachelor of Laws. When people wrote to him, they would put the abbreviation *Esq.* after his name, for *esquire*, a term of respect for attorneys.

3

At the Bar

Thurgood couldn't wait to start practicing law. At last, he would have the chance to put some of his ideas to work. He had no trouble passing the Maryland bar exam, which entitled him to practice law in that state. The term *bar* refers to the railing in a courtroom that separates the judge and the attorneys from the spectators. The bar exam is given to ensure that lawyers practicing in a state know that state's laws.

Thurgood also looked forward to making some money to help out his family. He knew that it had been a hardship on Buster and his parents to support him while he was at law school. He and Buster stayed in Baltimore after graduation. They continued to live with his parents until Thurgood could make enough money to afford a home of their own. He joined a small black law firm in Baltimore and looked forward to the time when he would make enough money to be independent.

But he found that he was bored with the divorce cases and claims against property that the firm handled. He couldn't even get excited about the many criminal cases that didn't touch upon the area of civil rights. The cases that interested him were civil rights cases, and what he really wanted to do, as he put it years later, was "straighten out all this business about civil rights." The trouble with such cases was that they usually failed in the courts and that the plaintiffs— the people who wanted to take their cases to court— had no money. Thurgood took many civil rights cases for free, but after a year he calculated that not only had he not made any money, he had actually lost about $1,000 in time and expenses. He was so short of money that he sometimes had to borrow from his secretary to buy lunch. This was no way to operate in the middle of the Great Depression.

To make matters worse, he wasn't even getting any respect for his efforts. His friends thought he was foolish to concentrate on cases that he couldn't hope to win. People in the community didn't seem to respect the fact that he was working for them. "Word got around that I was a free lawyer," Thurgood recalled many years later. "That does you no good." Still, Thurgood stuck stubbornly to civil rights law. His interest in the welfare of the black community in Baltimore led him to join various civic organizations, including the Baltimore branch of the National Association for the Advancement of Colored People (NAACP). He became friendly with other community activists such as Carl Murphy, publisher of the *Baltimore Afro-American*, and Lillie Jackson, who was active in community and church affairs. They referred civil rights cases to him. Eventually, he built up the largest law practice in Baltimore, but he still couldn't make a living.

In 1935 he at last got the chance to work on a case that he believed he had a chance of winning. His former professor, Charles Hamilton Houston, asked him to help on the case. The previous year, Houston had left Howard University to become chief counsel for the NAACP (usually pronounced N-double-A-C-P) at its headquarters in New York. His predecessors had been white attorneys.

The NAACP had been formed in 1909 by a group of black and white people who wanted to work together to fight an increase in white violence against blacks throughout the country, especially lynchings of blacks in the South. The organization conducted publicity campaigns and sought the support of state and national lawmakers. It also engaged in legal activities on the part of blacks, especially defending blacks accused of crimes. By 1926, the NAACP was paying more and more attention to the law.

It became involved in a challenge to the white pri-

mary election in Texas, in which blacks were not allowed to vote. Other cases had to do with school
segregation. Soon, so many cases were being brought
to the NAACP that it decided to launch a full-scale
campaign against legal injustices of all kinds. In 1935,
Charles Hamilton Houston was named to lead that
campaign. In turn, Houston naturally sought out the
young black attorneys that he had helped to groom at
Howard. In this particular case, a black student in
Maryland named Donald Murray had approached the
NAACP about gaining admittance to the all-white
University of Maryland Law School, and Houston
decided to take the case. Knowing that Thurgood was
practicing in Baltimore and remembering how hard
Thurgood had worked on William Hastie's North
Carolina case, Houston realized that Thurgood was a
natural to work on the case with him. Houston had
Thurgood named the NAACP's legal counsel in Baltimore. However, he cautioned Thurgood about putting too much energy into this and other NAACP
cases, saying: "I do not advise that you drop everything for NAACP work. Keep a finger on your office
practice whatever you do. You can get all the publicity
from the NAACP work but you have got to keep your
eye out for cashing in." But Thurgood Marshall would
find it very hard not to be single-minded in his devotion to civil rights cases, especially ones that he had a
chance of winning. It was his feeling that the NAACP
cases he was working on had that chance.

Donald Murray was a member of a prominent black

Baltimore family and a graduate of Amherst College in Massachusetts, which also happened to be Charles Houston's alma mater. He had applied to the University of Maryland Law School, but his application had been rejected. The state provided for black students who wanted to attend law school by offering scholarships to out-of-state universities to just fifty students. These scholarships were in the amount of $200. Murray knew that $200 was not enough to pay his way to an out-of-state law school, and he wanted to seek a court order to force the university's board of regents to admit him. That court order was filed in state court in April, and Murray prepared to enroll at the university in the fall. The university and the state appealed the court order. They also requested a quick hearing on the appeal so that the case could be decided before fall registration. The Maryland Court of Appeals denied the request.

Meanwhile, Murray was in financial trouble and did not have the necessary tuition even if by some chance he was admitted. So, while Thurgood worked on the legal case, he also worked on getting some financial help for his client. He got loans from Carl Murphy and from a black fraternity.

Next, Thurgood wanted to prepare a very detailed case that would cite any previous cases that were relevant. In that way, he believed, similar cases could be pursued in the future using the same basic brief. Charles Hamilton Houston studied the brief Thurgood had prepared and offered suggestions.

Thurgood and Houston presented the NAACP's arguments before the Maryland Court of Appeals in late 1935. Thurgood's father and Buster were present to watch proudly as he made his forceful arguments against Maryland's system of segregation in higher education. The state's attorneys tried to use the same argument that the University of North Carolina had used successfully—that the students paid tuition and so the university law school was a private institution. Thurgood pointed out that the law school had been private until 1920, when it had merged with the Maryland State College of Agriculture. In merging with a state school, it became an agency of the state. The Maryland Court of Appeals, in its opinion handed down in January 1936, held that the law school was clearly a public agency.

Attorneys for the state insisted that equal monies were spent on black and white higher education. Thurgood argued that a technical college for blacks was not equal to a law school for whites. The court agreed. The state argued that very few black students wanted to go to law school. Thurgood cited a recent Supreme Court decision in a completely unrelated case that held that it was the fact of discrimination not the number of people discriminated against that was important.

The court looked at the state's system of scholarships for students. A fund had been recently set up, and many observers believed it was established just to prevent blacks from trying to enter the University of

Maryland. The court found that the $200 provided by the fund would cover the cost of tuition at Howard University Law School but not the costs of commuting. Thus the state fell short of providing equal opportunity to Murray. The court gave Maryland the choice of opening a new law school for blacks or admitting Murray. The state had to admit Murray.

Thurgood, who had been the picture of dignity in court, let himself go the minute he got outside. He threw his arms over his head and danced around, wildly hugging his father and his wife. This victory was the first to have been won in the area of educational segregation, and Thurgood Marshall had reason to be proud.

So did Donald Murray, who'd had the courage to fight segregation at the University of Maryland Law School. But his fight could not stop there. Walter White, head of the NAACP, wrote to him just before he registered, saying: "Work hard, make the most brilliant record of which you are capable; conduct yourself with dignity and naturalness. By your very manner you will create, if you wish to do so, a new concept of the Negro in the minds of your fellow students and professors." It was an example of the double burden placed on black people in a white society. First, they had to get past barriers that whites never had to face. Once past those barriers, they had to be twice as good just to gain a little bit of respect.

Thurgood wanted to build on the victory in the Murray case, and soon he and Charles Houston were hard at work on other cases. As they traveled in the South, Thurgood's car became an office on wheels: "Charlie would sit in my car—I had a little old beat-up '29 Ford—and type out the briefs. And he could type up a storm—faster than any secretary—and not just two fingers. . . . We'd stay at friends' homes in those days, for free." Thurgood enjoyed working with Houston, but at the same time he was wondering how in the world he was going to make a living. He confided to Houston in May 1936, "Personally, I would not give up these cases here in Maryland for anything in the world, but at the same time there is no opportunity to get down to really hustling for business."

It occurred to Thurgood that he could make some steady income by teaching part-time at Howard University Law School, and he applied for a position there. But he really wanted to pursue his NAACP work full-time, and so he wrote to Houston in New York asking if he could be paid $150 a month for his NAACP work. Houston replied with an even better offer. He invited Thurgood to join him in New York as his assistant at the NAACP.

Many years later, Thurgood recalled his first impression of the national headquarters of the NAACP: "How very tush-tush. . . . It was Dr. Whosis and Mr. Whatsis and all kinds of nonsense like that, bowing and scraping like an embassy scene. . . . Well, I took a long look, not too long but long enough, and I figured I'd have to bust that stuff up pretty quick. Believe me, I had 'em talking first names in nothin' time and no more of that formality business. I was gonna relax and operate in my natural-born way and that's just what happened."

The salary that Thurgood would be making at the NAACP was not enough to finance a move to New York for him and Buster, so he traveled frequently from Baltimore to New York. It was hard on him and Buster, but both agreed that Thurgood's heart was in his NAACP work and that he should follow his heart. Also, by spending time in both cities, he could remain in the thick of the Maryland cases that he was pursuing.

Thurgood decided to fight discrimination in the Baltimore County public schools. In the county that surrounded Baltimore, there were no black high schools. Students had to attend high school in the city. They had to pay tuition unless they passed an entrance examination. If they passed, the state would pay the tuition through the eleventh grade, but not the twelfth, since the state didn't really want a lot of black students to graduate from high school. Unfortunately, only about one-third of the students who took the test passed. Thurgood brought two suits against the county. One was to force the city to admit all black students to the black high school there. The other was to force the county to integrate its white schools. He knew very well that he wouldn't win that one. He did succeed in getting the county to pay the tuition of black high-school students all the way through the twelfth grade, and that in itself was a major victory.

He was more successful in attacking the system under which black teachers in the state of Maryland were paid less than white teachers. In several instances, all he had to do was file a lawsuit, and a school board would come around. For example, in August 1937 a black teacher in Calvert County named Elizabeth Brown wrote to Thurgood asking for help and enclosing a copy of her record. Armed with her record alone, he was able to negotiate a settlement with Calvert County in four months.

While they welcomed such easy victories, Thurgood and the NAACP were concerned that they couldn't try a salary case in court. Only by having a court declare that unequal salaries were illegal could they hope to establish a legal precedent that would carry weight in similar cases. As long as school boards kept settling out of court, there could be no legal precedents established, and each case had to be pursued individually.

Meanwhile, Thurgood was spending so much time on these cases for the NAACP that he had little time for his private practice. He was not making enough money to live on. Still, he always presented an image of being well off. Thanks to Buster's help, the couple of suits he owned were always cleaned and well pressed, his shirts and handkerchiefs starched, his collars stiff. Even without Buster, he would have dressed well, for he felt that it was important to keep up his image. He realized that if he wanted people to respect his thoughts and words, he would have to dress in a way that would not detract from them. He knew that if he looked scruffy, people would think his intelligence was scruffy as well.

Roy Wilkins remembered Thurgood as being "Hollywood-handsome": "He wore natty, double-breasted suits with immaculate white handkerchiefs sticking out of the breast pocket; he had a neatly trimmed mustache and a way of wrinkling his brow. . . . He was from Baltimore, and his tactics combined a shrewd Southern way of leaving white foes enough rope to hang themselves with a Northern spare-me-the-sorghum style."

Thurgood's down-to-earth style and his shrewdness did not go unnoticed in the NAACP. In 1938, when Charles Hamilton Houston retired, Thurgood was named chief counsel for the NAACP in New York.

His new position came with a raise of $200 a year, which brought his annual salary to $2,600. To Thurgood, that seemed at first like a great deal of money. "When I came home to tell my wife, I was very carried away with the raise," Thurgood recalled, "And she said, 'Two hundred dollars?' I said, 'Yes.' She said, 'Not that I don't appreciate it, but how much is that a week?' " While it was less than four dollars a week more, Thurgood and Buster decided it was enough for them to afford a walk-up apartment in Harlem. Besides, now that Thurgood was chief counsel, he would not have much time to travel to Baltimore.

4

Thurgood Marshall
Before the Supreme Court

There was so much segregation and discrimination against black people, especially in the South, that Thurgood tried to be everywhere at once. A school desegregation case here, an unequal pay case there, a lynching case somewhere else—he tried to work on them all. Fortunately, the year following Thurgood's and Buster's move to New York, the NAACP legal staff became a separate organization, and Thurgood was elected director-counsel of the new Legal Defense and Education Fund. It was small and underfunded at first. The office had two rooms, and Thurgood shared it with his staff lawyer, Edward Dudley; research assistant Robert Carter; two secretaries; and a part-time volunteer named Constance Baker Motley, a student at Columbia University Law School, who would later become the nation's first black woman federal judge. Still, it was better than a one-man office.

As director-counsel of the NAACP, Thurgood was constantly traveling, often at risk to his own life. On one occasion, he and Walter White, executive director of the NAACP, disguised themselves as sharecroppers (black farmers who worked the land of white farmers in return for a share of the crop) to investigate a lynching on a plantation in Mississippi. If their real identities had been discovered, their lives would have been in grave danger, for they could easily have been lynched as well, just for trying to investigate a lynching. The attitude of many whites in the South was that any black who tried to fight against segregation deserved to be killed by a mob, and this attitude had been present for half a century. The NAACP had been campaigning against lynching since its beginnings, but nothing the organization had tried had made much difference. That is one reason why the NAACP had turned to a campaign to get the state and federal laws changed.

In later years, a black friend who was an undertaker took personal charge of his safety whenever he was in Mississippi. According to Thurgood, "He would bring one of his big Cadillacs with thirty rifles in the back and about three other men. Anybody who had any ideas, they got rid of 'em right quick."

After a while, because he had a limited staff and limited resources, Thurgood realized he had to be very careful about the cases he chose to pursue. He tried to concentrate on cases in which the law seemed quite clearly on the side of black people and which the NAACP had a good chance of winning.

One such case concerned unequal pay for black teachers in Norfolk, Virginia. In September 1939, Thurgood talked Melvin Alston—a teacher who was president of the local teacher's association—into suing in the federal courts. Thurgood eventually argued the case in front of the United States Court of Appeals for the Fourth Circuit. When the hearing was over, the three judges on the court paid Thurgood a rare compliment. Still in their robes, they stepped down off the bench to congratulate him on his presentation. Needless to say, Thurgood had won *Alston v. School Board.*

There were some cases in which he managed to get things done without having to go through all the local, state, and federal courts. For example, in Texas in the 1930s, black people were not allowed to serve on juries. Yet Texas law, not to mention federal law and the Constitution, clearly stated that people accused of crimes had the right to be tried by a jury of their *peers*, or people like themselves. So, Thurgood went to Austin, the capital of Texas, and made an appointment to see the governor, James Allred. He pointed out to the governor that not letting blacks serve on juries was a direct violation of Texas law. The governor listened to Thurgood's arguments and was won over. Not only did he vow to enforce the law from then on, he also told Thurgood that he'd see to it that the Texas Rangers helped protect blacks who did serve on jury duty.

But some cases were not so easily won. Thurgood and his staff, which grew each year, had to fight the same cases over and over in local, state, and district courts.

There are several levels to the American court system, which is set up so that people who think they have not gotten justice in one court can appeal to a higher one. There are local courts and state courts. If either the plaintiff or the defendant questions a decision handed down in one of these courts, the next step is to go to the federal court of appeals for that particular part of the country or district. Above these federal district courts are the circuit courts of appeals, and above them is the United States Supreme Court. Sometimes, Thurgood and the other NAACP lawyers took their cases all the way to the Supreme Court.

As director-counsel for the NAACP, Thurgood knew he would be arguing cases before the Supreme Court. He applied for permission to do so, and it was granted in 1939. Each year, many cases are presented to the Supreme Court, but if the justices believe the constitutional point in question has already been decided, they will decline to hear the case. Civil rights law did often require interpretation of the Constitution, and Thurgood found himself in front of the highest court in the land many times.

Months and sometimes years of preparation went

into each case that the NAACP took to the Supreme Court. Thurgood and his staff studied the Constitution over and over again. They studied all the court decisions in similar cases to find out about precedents. They worked hard to write briefs that would set forth their arguments clearly and convincingly. And they practiced appearing before the Supreme Court.

When attorneys argue cases before the Supreme Court, they stand at a podium in the center of the room and face the nine justices. One attorney for each side of the case makes his presentation, which can last no more than thirty minutes. Any justice may interrupt the attorney to ask questions, and the attorney must be prepared to answer these questions clearly and forcefully. In preparing to argue cases before the Court, Thurgood and the NAACP had one great advantage. Before a case went before the Court, there would be an all-day rehearsal at Howard University Law School.

Howard professors acted the parts of the nine justices, and each professor had studied the record and the personality of the judge he impersonated and tried to ask questions that the judge might ask. Unlike the real Supreme Court, in the Howard dry runs, law students sat in the audience and were encouraged to ask questions also. The aim of the dry run was to ask the toughest questions possible so that Thurgood would not face any surprises when he argued before the actual Supreme Court.

These dry runs at Howard were invaluable. In one

case, which had to do with fair housing, a student in the audience asked a question that no one could answer—not Thurgood and not the professors who were playing the parts of the justices. At the end of the session, a group of lawyers and professors met to try to answer the question. They pored over law books, they discussed the question far into the night. Finally, around dawn, they decided on the answer. When the case went before the Supreme Court, Justice Felix Frankfurter asked the very same question only minutes after the hearing began. Thanks to the dry run at Howard, Thurgood had the answer ready.

Thanks to his own intelligence and hard work and to the dry runs at Howard, more often than not Thurgood won his cases. One of the most important also concerned the state of Texas and the right of blacks to vote in Democratic Party primary elections. The Texas Democratic Party did not allow blacks to vote in primary elections, insisting that it was a private club. The same was true of most southern states. Thurgood and the NAACP felt they had a strong case in Texas. He argued that a political party that put up candidates for local and state offices could not be a private club. He argued that, as citizens, blacks were being deprived of their civil rights if they were not allowed to vote in the Democratic primaries. The Supreme Court heard arguments on both sides of this case, which was called *Smith v. Allright*, and decided in 1944 that the Texas white primaries were unconstitutional.

The Court's decision had a major impact on politics in the South and on voting rights for black people. It practically guaranteed black people the right to vote, although white racists in the South managed to find other ways to keep blacks from voting, such as poll taxes. These were taxes that voters had to pay once a year and that many poor black people could not afford to pay. In some areas of the South, these poll taxes were not eliminated until the passage of the federal Voting Rights Act of 1965.

Another case that Thurgood won in the U.S. Supreme Court was *Morgan v. Virginia*. The state of Virginia insisted that black and white passengers be segregated not only on buses that traveled within the state lines but also on interstate buses. Thus, a black passenger who boarded a southbound interstate bus in Pennsylvania could sit anywhere he wanted until the bus reached the Virginia line. At that point, he would have to move to the back of the bus. The Supreme Court ruled that interstate buses were subject to federal law not the laws of the states through which they passed. Since federal law forbade segregation, interstate buses could not be segregated. Commenting on the Court's decision, Thurgood said it was "a decisive blow to the evil of segregation and all that it stands for."

Many of the cases Thurgood argued had to do not so much with changing laws as with saving people. One such case occurred in Mississippi, where three cotton-field workers named Ed Brown, Yank Ellington, and Henry Shields had been sentenced to death for the ax murder of a white farmer named Raymond Stewart. John A. Clark, a white lawyer who had been assigned by the court to represent the three blacks, appealed to the NAACP for help.

There was no evidence linking the three suspects to the crime except for three "confessions" that had been beaten out of the suspects. Bloodhounds at the scene had not turned up any scent. While the police claimed to have found a bloody ax and bloodstained clothing, they were unable to produce that evidence in court. Still, the local court took just one day to charge the three men, and it took that court just one day to try the men and condemn them to death.

Many court-appointed white attorneys would have washed their hands of the case once a verdict was reached, feeling that they had done their duty. But John A. Clark was a southern white lawyer with a conscience, and he knew that his clients had not received justice. He appealed the verdict to the Mississippi Supreme Court. A majority of the court upheld the conviction. But one judge did not go along with the majority. This gave Clark hope that the verdict might be reversed in a higher court. But by this time he was receiving death threats from whites who did not want to see justice for blacks. That's when he turned to the NAACP.

In his letter to the NAACP, Clark wrote, "I believe these men have been tortured to make them confess and that confession is the only evidence against them, but I cannot carry this case any further. It's so bad that I think it would be well if your organization would come in and help them."

NAACP lawyers went to Mississippi. Just thirty-six hours before the three men were scheduled to be executed, the NAACP got a stay, or delay, of execution. Then Thurgood took the case to the U.S. Supreme Court.

The Supreme Court reversed the convictions. Chief Justice Charles Evans Hughes wrote the Court's opinion, saying, "It would be difficult to conceive of methods more revolting to the sense of justice than those taken to procure the confessions."

But the case was not over yet. The chief justice of the Mississippi Supreme Court refused to release the men. Meanwhile, the police set about finding "new evidence" against them. Fearing that they would be wrongly convicted a second time, the men agreed to plead guilty to a lesser charge, and in return were given reduced sentences.

A case that Thurgood did not win in the Supreme Court also had to do with a murder. In 1939 W. D. Lyons, a young black man in Hugo, Oklahoma, was arrested and accused of the murder of the Rogers, a poor white farming couple and their four-year-old son. He was kept in jail for eleven days and beaten until he confessed to the crime. A few days later, he signed a second confession. The arresting officers had not had an arrest warrant when they arrested Lyons. He had not had a lawyer to talk to when he signed either confession. It was more than eight months between the time Lyons was arrested for the murder and the time he was formally charged with it.

Finally, a lawyer named Stanley Belden agreed to take Lyons' case. He immediately contacted Thurgood in New York, who arrived in Hugo three weeks before the trial was due to start. He was unprepared for the situation that he found. The crime had stirred up a lot of emotion in Hugo. The white family had not only been murdered, but their house had been set on fire afterward so that their bodies had been badly burned. Many whites in Hugo could not wait to see Lyons convicted for the crime and executed.

The small black community in Hugo were equally convinced that Lyons had been *railroaded*, that the police had been more concerned with arresting someone than with arresting the real killer. They were concerned that the life of the important NAACP lawyer from New York might be in danger, and they were determined to protect him. Thurgood arrived to find that they had worked out an elaborate plan. He would eat in a different house each evening and sleep in yet another house each night. A small group had armed themselves and would be his bodyguards. Thurgood had not been worried about his safety while on his way to Hugo. Now, hearing of the elaborate precautions to protect him, he started to be afraid.

After about a week, he was tired of so much protection. So much moving around kept him from concentrating on the case. He thanked the concerned black citizens of Hugo, but said he would prefer to take his chances. No attempts were made on his life. In fact, many whites in the town had developed a grudging respect for him. He carried himself with great dignity, and knew the law inside and out. James Nabrit, a fellow NAACP attorney, once said of him: "I've been all over the country with Thurgood, and I've never known any situation where after two or three days he was not liked by the very people he was opposing. I believe it is almost his most important contribution because everywhere he has gone he has made friends for us."

At the trial, Thurgood and Belden pointed out many problems with the state's case against Lyons. They tried to prove that Lyons had only confessed because he had been beaten by the police. They pointed out that the one "witness"—the Rogers' eight-year-old son, who had escaped before the killer could get him, too—had not seen the face of the killer. All he had seen was "a black hand."

The police said they had "found" the murder weapon, an ax, in the ruins of the house three weeks after the murder. But a local man testified that he had carefully raked through the ruins of the house the morning after the fire and had found no ax.

Even Mrs. Rogers' father testified for Lyons, stating that one of the policemen had told him he had beaten a confession out of Lyons. But the all-white jury found Lyons guilty of the murder anyway.

Thurgood appealed the conviction to the state

Court of Appeals, but that court denied the appeal. He then took the case to the Supreme Court, but in spite of all the evidence to the contrary, the majority of the Court ruled that Lyons had been given a fair trial. W. D. Lyons was not executed, but he spent decades in jail for a crime that he insisted he did not commit.

Thurgood felt very badly for having lost that case. For a while he felt bitter about the way the justice system could be used so unjustly. But he realized that being bitter was a waste of time. He had to keep on fighting. The whole system of justice in the United States was like a brick wall erected against black people. The only way to tear down that wall, at least for the time being, was to knock it apart, brick by brick. If a brick proved too strong to knock out, then the best thing to do was to go after another brick.

5

The War Years:
A Different Kind of Battle

In the early 1940s, Thurgood found himself fighting on a new front. World War II was raging in Europe, and the army put out a call for thirty thousand pilots a year. Blacks hoped that maybe a new branch of the United States Army would not be segregated.

An engineering student at Howard University named Yancey Williams heard about the new Army Air Corps and decided he would like to be an army pilot. He already had a pilot's license. When the army turned him down, he sought the help of the NAACP. Thurgood represented Williams and managed to make a small crack in the barrier against blacks in the military. The army agreed to train thirty-three black pilots to become the Ninety-ninth Pursuit Squadron. A special training school was set up at Tuskegee Institute, a black college in Alabama. After the United States entered the fighting in World War II, the Ninety-ninth Pursuit Squadron proved to be so good in battle that a second group, the Hundredth Pursuit Squadron, was formed.

The United States officially entered World War II after the Japanese bombed the U.S. naval base at Pearl Harbor, Hawaii, on December 7, 1941. Soon it was fighting not only against Japan in the Pacific but also with its European allies against Hitler's forces. Many young men were drafted, and many men and women went to work in the busy war hardware factories. Blacks encountered segregation in both fighting and making materials for the war effort.

The military had instituted a draft before the United States had entered the war. In a draft, every young man must sign up for military service and be available if and when he is called. In this way, the armed forces can muster a fighting force quickly. At the time, the armed forces were highly segregated. The only military jobs available for blacks were menial, like mess (food) attendants and ditch diggers and latrine cleaners. Thus, the draft that was instituted was a Jim Crow draft. Young black and white men signed up separately so that there would be no mistakes made when the army, for example, needed combat troops. In that case, it went to the white list of eligible men. When it needed ditch diggers, it went to the black list.

Since there were no separate black military training camps, black recruits were trained at white training camps, which were mostly in the South. These were rigidly segregated: Black soldiers traveled on separate buses, bought cigarettes and candy at separate counters, and attended separate movie theaters on base.

Also, even before the United States was at war, its factories were working around the clock to supply war materials to its European allies. This meant more jobs, but at first black workers were turned away from many American factories.

A. Philip Randolph, president of the Brotherhood of Sleeping Car Porters, the first black union, called for a March on Washington, D.C., in protest. His idea was to get ten thousand black workers to march down Pennsylvania Avenue to demonstrate for defense jobs and dignity. Randolph, who was also a member of the NAACP, had a great reputation for organizing. President Franklin D. Roosevelt realized that he could organize such a march. He knew, too, that Randolph's cause was just. So, to prevent the march, the president issued Executive Order 8802 barring discrimination by race, color, creed, or national origin in any defense plant that received contracts from the federal government. Only then did Randolph call off the march.

Southern blacks flocked to the North, where most large factories were located, and it wasn't long before tensions between the races produced explosions. In 1943 there was a series of riots, in Los Angeles, Detroit, Michigan, and Harlem, as well as in the southern cities of Mobile, Alabama, and Beaumont, Texas. In every case, many more blacks than whites were killed and injured, often by white police. In the case of the

Detroit riot, seventeen blacks were killed by white policemen. The police said they had simply shot looters who took advantage of the unrest to steal goods from stores. But Thurgood went to Detroit to investigate for himself and found that many of the shootings had been random.

Tensions only increased as more and more blacks were called to active combat duty in the war. As the war continued, the War Department was forced to be less choosy about whom it drafted. Many blacks did not wait to be drafted but enlisted on their own. More and more were given the opportunity to enter combat, and many distinguished themselves in battle. But when the war was over and they got back home, black veterans were unwilling to accept the same segregated conditions that they had left. After all, what was the point of fighting for the freedom of Europeans when they did not enjoy that same freedom at home? What was the difference between a bench in Germany that was marked "Juden" (meaning for Jews) and a bench in the American South that was marked "colored"?

In the South, returning black soldiers carried themselves with a new pride, and white southerners worried that they would get "uppity." It became dangerous for a black soldier to appear in public in uniform, because uniformed black soldiers frequently were shot by southern police. In Columbia, Tennessee, in February 1946, a nineteen-year-old black man named James Stephenson, who had served for three years in the navy, was arrested and charged with assault. He had gone with his mother to a repair shop to complain about poor repair work on a radio. When Mrs. Stephenson complained, the white repairman hit her. Her son, in turn, hit the repairman.

The white community of Columbia was soon up in arms about the incident. A mob of men went to the jailhouse and demanded that the sheriff hand over Stephenson. But the sheriff had had sense enough to get Stephenson out of town. Denied their main victim, the mob considered what to do next.

Meanwhile, the black community was afraid the mob would turn on them. They armed themselves and waited. That night, four white policemen went into the black neighborhood. The residents thought they were the advance guard of the mob and opened fire. All four policemen were wounded.

A few hours later, the local police, the state highway patrol, and the Tennessee National Guard descended on Columbia's black neighborhood. They broke into the black businesses and nearly destroyed them, tearing up the chairs in the barbershop, scattering the doctor's instruments, breaking up the tables in the pool hall. Then they set out on a house-to-house search for weapons, herding residents out of their homes with their hands up, and arresting a total of 106.

As soon as Thurgood heard about what had happened, he went to Columbia to assist in defending the 106 black people who had been arrested. Also on the side of the defense were a white lawyer from Chattanooga, Tennessee, named Maurice Weaver, and a West Indian lawyer named Z. Alexander Looby, who lived in Nashville and was a member of the NAACP's National Legal Committee.

The first thing the three lawyers did was to request a *change of venue* to get the trials moved away from Columbia. They argued successfully that emotions in Columbia were so high that the defendants could never get a fair trial. The judge in the case moved the trials to Lawrenceburg, a small town about fifty miles away. It was not Columbia, but it was hardly a good place for the trials of black people. A sign at the Lawrenceburg city limits read: NIGGER, READ AND RUN. DON'T LET THE SUN GO DOWN ON YOU HERE. IF YOU CAN'T READ, RUN ANYWAY.

Lawrenceburg was not a place for an interracial group of lawyers to be after dark. So the three attorneys stayed in Nashville and made a round trip of more than two hundred miles every day. But that didn't stop local white racists from making threats upon their lives. For Thurgood, it was one of the most dangerous situations he'd been in in years, but he refused to allow his fear for his own safety to get in the way of what he knew he had to do. He and the others argued forcefully on behalf of the defendants, and miraculously, the jury proved sympathetic. Only two defendants were found guilty. The rest were acquitted.

While he was delighted with the verdict, Thurgood knew that Lawrenceburg, Tennessee, was no place in which to celebrate. He would have loved to have a drink with his fellow attorneys, but they had all agreed long before that they would not drink in Lawrenceburg. Thurgood had even taken the extra precaution of frequently searching the car to make sure no liquor had been planted. As soon as the trial was over, Thurgood and the two lawyers on his team headed for Nashville. Thurgood was driving. They had just crossed a bridge when their way was blocked by a car in the middle of the highway. Thurgood blew the car horn, and when the other car did not move, he drove around it on the shoulder of the road. As soon as he got back on the road, he heard a siren. A highway patrolman pulled them over and announced that he had a warrant to search for whiskey. Finding none, the highway patrolman let the three attorneys go.

A few miles down the road, another policeman stopped them. This one decided that Thurgood was drunk and ordered him into his patrol car. He told Weaver and Looby that they could go, but they were not about to leave their friend. They followed the patrol car as it headed for the Duck River. No one knows what might have happened to Thurgood if they had not stuck with him. He would not have been the first black man to have gone off in a southern patrol car, never to be seen or heard from again. Eventually, the patrol car, aware of its escort, headed for Columbia.

At the Columbia courthouse, Thurgood was taken before the local magistrate, who just happened to be a nondrinker and who claimed to be able to tell in an instant if a man was drinking just by smelling his breath. "The magistrate was a short man," Thurgood recalled about ten years later, "and I put my hands on his shoulders and rocked back and forth, breathing as hard as I could into that man's face." The magistrate announced, "This man isn't drunk, he hasn't even had a drink." He ordered the officers to release him. Thurgood rejoined his friends in the waiting car, keenly aware of how close he had come to an untimely death. "I really hadn't had anything to drink," he recalled, "but after leaving there we drove to Nashville and then, boy, I *really* wanted a drink."

If anything had happened to Thurgood, the NAACP and black people would have lost one of their most tireless defenders. By the late 1940s, there were enough other well-trained black attorneys so that the NAACP could have filled Thurgood's job. But few other men would have had his energy and commitment, not to mention his physical stamina and emotional stability. He worked killing hours and sometimes passed out from hard work and lack of sleep. "This life is something," he said one day. "You never know when you're going to meet yourself coming around the corner." But he usually managed to keep his sense of humor. "Isn't it nice," he said once, "that nobody cares which twenty-three hours of the day I work." On long train rides, he would hang out with the dining car waiters, laughing and joking about his summers working on the B&O Railroad. He had such a fondness for trains that one Christmas his friends gave him an electric train set and a striped engineer's cap. He happily called all the neighborhood children in to watch his train run around the track.

At the NAACP office, he would sometimes take over the switchboard when the operator went to lunch, taking great delight at the confusion of callers who had not expected him to answer the telephone personally. He rarely had time for a private life with Buster. But through it all he remained calm and dignified and alert. Roy Wilkins later wrote, "The broadest shoulders of all belonged to Thurgood," by which he meant that of all the officeholders in the NAACP Thurgood carried the greatest burden in the fight for equal rights for black people.

At any one time in the late 1940s, Thurgood had hundreds of cases to watch over or take part in. Sadly, for black people and for America, some of these cases had to do with the same issues as cases he had previously won. The Supreme Court already had decided against white primaries in the South in *Smith v. Allright*, but that didn't mean that black people could now vote in southern primaries. South Carolina, for example, had responded by doing away with all laws on its primaries. That way, the Supreme Court could not say the laws were unconstitutional. Other states— including Alabama, Georgia, Mississippi, and Florida—continued to deny blacks the right to vote in Democratic primaries. They found clever ways to get around the Supreme Court ruling, proving yet again that American law is so subject to interpretation and so careful to guard states' rights against federal power that citizens often suffer.

But the mood of the country, even in the South, was beginning to change. It was becoming a little bit harder to out-and-out deny blacks their civil rights. After the state of South Carolina repealed all of its primary laws—and still refused blacks the right to vote in the primaries—a black man named George Elmore decided to sue the state. Thurgood handled the case for the NAACP. He argued on behalf of Elmore in federal district court and won. The state appealed this decision to federal circuit court, but once again Elmore won. Thurgood and other black fighters for equal rights were thankful that fair-minded judges were now sitting on the benches of some southern courts.

Even after the war, Thurgood continued to fight for the rights of black soldiers, at home and abroad. In the early 1950s, American soldiers were stationed in Japan, as an occupying force over a beaten nation, and in South Korea, where the United States had been asked to help in the fight against the North Korean communists. When black soldiers complained of mistreatment on the part of their superior officers, Thurgood traveled to the Far East to investigate. He pursued witnesses wherever he could find them, including the front lines. "There was so much sniper fire that you couldn't even go to the bathroom without a buddy, and then one of us had to take rifles," he said years later. One day he was walking with his escort,

Colonel D. D. Martin, when they heard rifle fire. Both dived into the nearest ditch. "Where are you, Marshall?" yelled Martin. "Are you kidding?" Thurgood called back. "I'm under you." Working on behalf of forty black soldiers who had been arrested on various charges, he got the sentences reduced for twenty-two of them.

While Thurgood was a tireless worker, at times the load became too much for him. He had been hospitalized from exhaustion brought on by overwork in 1946, and his doctors warned him that he could have a relapse if he didn't pace himself. He did the best he could, realizing that there was much left to be done, but there were times when he could not afford to slow down. In 1952, Buster remarked: "He's aged so in the past five years. His disposition's changed—he's nervous now where he used to be calm. This work is taking its toll of him. You know, it's a discouraging job he's set for himself."

6

Against "Separate
but Equal" Education

In slavery times, in many states it was illegal to teach slaves to read and write. Ever since, black people had believed that if they could only get a good education, they would be able to break down many of the barriers that were placed in front of them. They could get better jobs, enter more of the professions, and gain more respect from the white community. Once they had this respect, they believed that they might be able to break down the barriers of segregation.

But a good education was hard to get for black people. In every case of "separate but equal" schools, the black schools were separate but not equal. In many areas of the South, black schools were housed in black churches that had no heat or plumbing, while whites had their own brick schools with glass windows and central heating and running water. Black children had to walk to school, no matter how far away the black schools were. White children who did not live within walking distance of their schools were able to ride school buses. Black schools got used books from the white schools. Black schools did not have gym or music equipment, but white schools did. Black teachers were paid less than white teachers. The black school year was shorter than the white school year. Most black elementary schools were in session only five months so that the children could work in the fields from early spring until late fall. White schools were in session eight or nine months of the year.

Most southern towns had white high schools. Few southern towns had black high schools. Black students who wished to go to high school had to go to the nearest large city, which sometimes was not very near at all. And black students who wanted to go to white colleges were sent out of state rather than admitted.

For many years, the NAACP had concentrated only on proving that separate black schools were not equal. They did not try to attack the very notion of separate but equal as unconstitutional. They had good reason for not making an all-out attack on segregation. In the 1920s, 1930s, and early 1940s, the climate of the country was against any hint of integration.

By 1945, however, Thurgood and the other NAACP lawyers felt that the time had come to launch a direct attack on segregation. World War II had ended, and many black pilots and soldiers had distinguished themselves in the fighting. Many white people, especially in the North, believed that it was wrong to discriminate against blacks. Of these white people, some genuinely believed that segregation was wrong. Some others were more concerned with how the rest of the world viewed segregation in the United States. Communism, which had arisen in Russia, was taking hold in many parts of the world. It stood for equality of opportunity and for the rights of workers against big business. In the United States, the Communist Party enjoyed popularity among some white workers and intellectuals and among some black people. Communists, both in the United States and abroad, charged that the United States talked about but did not practice democracy. Some Americans realized that there was no way to argue against that charge, not when so many of its citizens were clearly being discriminated against.

President Harry S. Truman, who became president upon the death of President Franklin D. Roosevelt, began to take steps against discrimination. In December 1946, he set up a President's Commission on Civil Rights "to determine whether and in what respect . . . the authority and means possessed by the federal, state and local governments may be strengthened and improved to safeguard the civil rights of the people." The following June, he spoke at the NAACP's thirty-eighth annual convention, the first president to do so. "We must make the federal government a friendly, vigilant defender of the rights and equalities of all Americans," he said. "And again, I mean *all* Americans." In 1948, he issued Executive Order 9981 ending segregation in the U.S. armed forces.

Thurgood felt that with the president on the side of civil rights, it was time to push aggressively for them. But Thurgood had to consider how the rest of the leadership—not to mention the membership—of the NAACP wanted to proceed. The organization was growing; by the end of the war there were five hundred thousand members and twelve hundred branches. The treasury, swollen from membership dues and private contributions, was huge, and by 1947 the budget was over $319,000. But many of the organization's leaders and members were not ready for bold steps. Thurgood did not want to bring about a split in the organization, so he did not directly go after cases that would call segregation into question. Instead, he concentrated, as he had before, on small victories that would advance the cause of integration an inch or so each time. The legal precedent established in *Plessy v. Ferguson* had to be broken down. The fact that *separate* could never be *equal* had to be proved again and again in as many areas of American life as possible.

Thurgood could have concentrated on cases that would have won the right for black soldiers and other black people to sit anywhere they wanted on buses or to enter any restaurant they wanted. But unequal educaton was what bothered black people most, and that is the area on which Thurgood and the NAACP continued to concentrate.

They began with graduate schools. Here the issues were very clear-cut. If a state had no law school for blacks and would not admit blacks to its white law school, then it was clearly discriminating. There were many such cases that the NAACP could choose to take on. But they had to choose their cases very carefully. They had to involve very clear violations of students' rights, and the students themselves had to be beyond reproach. It would do no good to defend the rights of a student who had an arrest record, for example. Even if he had just as much right to attend graduate school as a student without a record, opposing attorneys could question his character and muddy the issue. The student plaintiff would also have to be willing to put up with a great deal of publicity, to face the possibility of death threats from whites who were against any kind of integration, and to have the patience necessary to wait out the months, and sometimes years, during which such a case could drag on. Thurgood and his staff looked long and hard for just the right cases.

By the middle 1940s, they had two cases, one in Oklahoma and one in Texas. In 1945, Ada Lois Sipuel, a junior at the State College for Negroes in Langston, Oklahoma, applied to the University of Oklahoma Law School and was rejected because she was black. She then went to the NAACP for help. In those days, it was fairly unusual for a woman to be willing to go through all that such a court case involved, but Ada Lois Sipuel was an unusual woman. Although she was married, she used her maiden name; very few women did that in the 1940s.

In April 1946 the case went before the state trial court, which dismissed the action. Sipuel appealed, and a year later the state supreme court affirmed the lower court's decision. Meanwhile, some students at the University of Oklahoma Law School supported her. An editorial in a student newspaper at the school stated that "separate school systems are impractical, undesirable, and unnecessary."

Thurgood took the case to the U.S. Supreme Court. In his arguments on Sipuel's behalf, he directly attacked the *Plessy v. Ferguson* decision, which had declared separate but equal accommodations constitutional. The Supreme Court decided in Sipuel's favor. The Court, in its decision, did not refer to the *Plessy v. Ferguson* ruling or to the constitutionality of the separate but equal doctrine. It did order the state of Oklahoma to act, and quickly, to provide Sipuel with the education she wanted. It could either admit her to the white school, close the white school, or open a black law school. Oklahoma did open a black law school, but in the eighteen months it operated, only one student attended. Sipuel did not apply, feeling that the black school could not possibly provide an education equal to the white school's. After the black school closed for lack of students, Sipuel was at last admitted to the white school. She entered in 1949 and graduated in 1951.

Meanwhile, black students in Oklahoma were applying to other graduate programs at the University of Oklahoma. All were rejected. One, George McLaurin, a black teacher in his sixties who wanted to get a doctorate in education, sued. A state court directed the university to admit him, which it did, but under very segregated conditions.

Every course for which he signed up was relocated to a classroom that had some sort of small alcove on the side. That is where McLaurin had to sit, away from the other students. Wherever he went—to the library, to the cafeteria—he had to sit in separate chairs and at separate tables. He sued again, and this case went all the way to the Supreme Court. The Court ruled that setting McLaurin apart imposed a handicap on him, and it ordered that the state remove all restrictions against McLaurin as a student.

While he was pursuing that case, Thurgood was hard at work on the Texas case. The plaintiff in that case was Heman Sweatt. He was a letter carrier for the post office who had wanted his employer to promote him to a clerical position. When he did not get the promotion, he felt that it was because of his race. He decided to go to law school so he could defend himself and other black people against discrimination. The University of Texas Law School denied him admission on the basis of his race, and Sweatt sued.

The state of Texas hurriedly set up a black law school consisting of two rooms and one part-time instructor. Sweatt went to the NAACP for help, and the NAACP sued the state again. This time the state set up the black law school on the grounds of the state university, gave its students access to the state law library (though not the white university law library), and arranged for white faculty to teach at the school.

It was now hard for Sweatt and the NAACP to argue that the separate facilities were not equal. But Thurgood saw an opportunity to broaden his arguments and attack the doctrine of separate but equal. He felt he could argue convincingly that the students at the black law school did not enjoy the same facilities or opportunities as the students at the white school. These included a law review, which was a publication about the law, and a moot court, a practice court in which students of law argue cases to get practice. Then there were less tangible things, such as reputation and the opportunity to develop professional contacts. "So," wrote Thurgood to William Hastie, his adviser and former professor, "whether we want it or not, we are now faced with the proposition of going into the question of segregation as such. I think we should do so because even if we don't take the case far, we at least should experiment on the type of evidence which we may be able to produce on this question."

Hastie advised him to be cautious, but Thurgood decided to go ahead anyway. It was time, he felt, to begin to attack segregation.

He sought evidence that was not just from law books. He read and quoted from sociological studies in his brief. One of these had been written by a Swedish sociologist named Gunnar Myrdal. Titled *An American Dilemma*, it criticized the United States for not living up to its promise of equality and showed how deeply segregation had hurt black people and denied them the chance to be equal citizens. He read and quoted surveys on how few black Americans held higher education degrees.

Meanwhile, a group of white students at the University of Texas formed an all-white branch of the NAACP, and there were demonstrations on campus in support of Sweatt. But the state of Texas and the university would not be swayed. Nor was the state court influenced. It rejected Sweatt's case.

Thurgood took this case to the Supreme Court, too, and won. In the majority opinion, Chief Justice Vinson wrote that he found it "difficult to believe that one who had a free choice between the law schools would consider the question close." By admitting blacks to a segregated law school, the state denied them contact with "most of the lawyers, witnesses, jurors, judges and other officials with whom petitioner will inevitably be dealing" as a lawyer. No education under those conditions could be "substantially equal" to that in the University of Texas Law School.

The Supreme Court decisions in the *McLaurin* and *Sweatt* cases were milestones. For the first time, the Court had broadened the idea of separate but equal to include more than physical facilities such as buildings and desks and chairs. In rendering its decisions, it had considered more intangible things and had taken into account sociological evidence. Thurgood was thrilled. It was now time to launch a direct attack on all aspects of "separate but equal" education in elementary and secondary schools, not just the physical ones.

Sadly, Charles Hamilton Houston did not live to see these milestones occur. On April 20, 1950, he died at the age of fifty-four. Thurgood was a pallbearer at his funeral. He hoped that his late friend and mentor had died secure in the knowledge that the men he had trained would carry on the fight in a way that would make him proud.

In late June 1950, three weeks after the *Sweatt* and *McLaurin* decisions, Thurgood convened a conference of lawyers to "map . . . the legal machinery" for an "all-out attack" on segregation. At the end of the conference, Thurgood announced, "We are going to insist on nonsegregation in American public education from top to bottom—from law school to kindergarten." The conference developed a resolution, which was approved by the NAACP Board of Directors in July 1950, stating that all future education cases would seek "education on a non-segregated basis and that no relief other than that will be acceptable."

It was a landmark in the history of the NAACP and the civil rights struggle. The resolution signaled a whole new attitude about the place of black people in American society. Before, the NAACP had waged its fight against *physical* segregation—for example, against separate schools that were not equal in facilities and resources and teacher salaries. Now, the fight would be to prove that separate facilities by their very nature could never be equal. It was a campaign for integration, although no one was about to risk saying that word.

Thurgood was glad that the resolution was adopted since, in fact, he and other NAACP lawyers were already pursuing just that strategy.

7

Brown v. Board of Education

In 1948, a schoolteacher and minister in Clarendon County, South Carolina, named J. A. DeLaine organized the black community to protest the fact that black children were deprived of bus transportation that was provided for white children. The lawsuit brought by the community was dismissed. Almost a year later, DeLaine met with Thurgood, who persuaded him that a full-scale attack on all inequalities made more sense than just a lawsuit about buses. The larger lawsuit was filed in November 1949.

Around the same time, another case arose in Topeka, Kansas, where seven-year-old Linda Brown had to cross railroad tracks to wait for a rattletrap bus to take her to her black school. There was a white school close by, and her father, the Reverend Oliver Brown, decided to sue the local school board to gain admittance to the white school for his daughter. This was the case that came to be known as *Brown v. Board of Education.*

Two other cases were in progress in Virginia and Delaware. In the Virginia case, the black community of Prince Edward County wanted the school board to build a new black high school to replace an old, overcrowded building. When the school board hemmed and hawed, the black students called a strike. Oliver Hill and Spottswood Robinson, two local NAACP attorneys, met with the students and told them that the NAACP would support a desegregation case but not a lawsuit aimed only at getting a new high school. The community agreed.

The NAACP wanted to direct its time, money, and energy toward the big issue of school desegregation. It did not want to get bogged down in minor issues. Thus, when a black mother in Delaware wanted the school bus for white children to stop and pick up her daughter as well, the NAACP wasn't much interested in pursuing the case. Louis Redding, the local NAACP lawyer, told her that he would not help her in that small matter, but if she was willing to bring a desegregation suit, he would help her all the way. She agreed.

By the late 1940s and early 1950s, Thurgood and his national NAACP legal office had the ability to coordinate four major lawsuits in South Carolina, Kansas, Virginia, and Delaware. Thurgood personally supervised the South Carolina suit, but he had able attorneys in the other states to supervise those suits.

By this time, the national office had developed a framework for desegregation arguments that included a great deal of psychological and sociological evidence. In the law school cases, this evidence had been presented by experts in the legal profession. For the elementary and high-school cases, they simply had to find experts in child psychology.

The cases in Kansas, Virginia, and South Carolina went against the NAACP. The only win came in Delaware, where the court found that facilities for black children were basically unequal and ordered desegregation. Thurgood and his staff were not surprised, for of the four states, Delaware was the least rigidly segregated. But now they had the opportunity to appeal the three decisions that had gone against them. In June 1952, the U.S. Supreme Court agreed to hear the appeal of both the Kansas and South Carolina cases. The hearing was set for December 9, 1952.

Thurgood forcefully and, he hoped, successfully argued the cases before the Supreme Court. He was surprised when the Court could not come to a decision. Instead, the Court asked that the cases be reargued and handed both sides a list of questions concerning the historical background of the Fourteenth Amendment and the probable effects if the Court happened to outlaw segregation.

Thurgood realized that this chance to reargue the cases and to answer the Court's questions offered the best chance black people had ever had to get *Plessy v. Ferguson* struck down and segregation outlawed. For this major breakthrough, he would have to call on more resources than Howard University could offer. In addition to calling on the best legal minds in the NAACP, he called together seventy-five experts, white and black, in the fields of history, economics, psychology, sociology, and education. They included William H. Kilpatrick of Columbia Teachers College in New York; Elsa E. Robinson, a highly respected psychologist at New York University; Joseph Banks Rhine, a psychologist at Duke University; and a psychologist from the University of California named David Krech. At their own expense, they met in New York in September 1953 to thrash out the answers. They explored every aspect of the Fourteenth Amendment and states' rights versus federal rights. The experts in child psychology talked about the effects of segregation on black children—the "intangibles" that Thurgood had used so successfully in arguing the graduate-school cases.

One of the experts in child psychology whose advice Thurgood sought was Dr. Kenneth B. Clark, the first black full professor at the City College of New York, who with his wife, Mamie Phipps Clark, had conducted a very important experiment back in 1940. They had tested black children's views of themselves in Philadelphia, Boston, and Worcester, Massachusetts, and several cities in Arkansas by using four dolls dressed in diapers and identical except for one thing: Two were pink and two were brown. They had shown the dolls to black children ages three to seven years and then measured the children's reactions to them based on the children's responses to a series of requests and questions.

First, they had said, "Give me the white doll" or "Give me the colored doll" or "Give me the Negro doll." Three-quarters of the children had correctly identified the dolls. Then, they said, "Give me the doll you like to play with," or "Give me the doll you like best," or "Give me the doll that is the nice doll," or "Give me the doll that looks bad," or "Give me the doll that is a nice color." The majority of the black children tested showed "an unmistakable preference for the white doll and a rejection of the brown doll." That was true even of the three-year-olds.

The Clarks were thus able to prove that black children had a very poor self-image. They were not proud of the way they looked. They wanted to be white.

Thurgood wanted to apply the results of the Clarks' experiment to the issue of segregation as a way of showing that segregation only increased black children's sense of inferiority. So he called Dr. Clark and asked if he would do the same experiment with children in Clarendon, South Carolina. With Thurgood and NAACP attorney Robert Carter, Clark rode a train south and tested sixteen black children, ages six to nine, at Scott's Branch, a joint black elementary and junior high school. Ten of the children said they liked the white doll better. Eleven of them added that the black doll looked bad. When asked, "Now show me the doll that's most like you," many of the children became upset when they had to point out the same doll that they had rejected. For Thurgood, this was definite proof that southern black children saw themselves as inferior.

After the conference ended, Thurgood and a few experts and lawyers who volunteered to continue working on the case boiled down the conference results to a thorough, 235-page brief, which was filed with the Supreme Court that November. Not long afterward, and before Thurgood was to present his arguments before the highest court in the land, Howard University Law School held a mock Supreme Court hearing on the case. When it was over, Thurgood was satisfied that he had built the strongest case possible. Now all he could do was hope and pray that the nine white justices on the U.S. Supreme Court would agree.

Waiting outside the Supreme Court chamber on the day the Court opened hearings on the case, Thurgood was very nervous, as he usually was before testifying before the Supreme Court. But as usual, once he entered the chamber and stood at the bar, he relaxed and spoke in confident tones. He spoke as if he was having a conversation with the nine judges and spoke not in legal technicalities but in clear, simple language that everyone in the overflowing chamber could understand.

Thurgood's opponents were some of the best lawyers in the nation. They included eighty-one-year-old John W. Davis, the solicitor general. The solicitor general is the federal government's attorney—and the federal government of President Dwight Eisenhower was against school desegregation. Davis was recognized as the country's leading authority on the Constitution. Arguing on behalf of the Topeka, Kansas, Board of Education, as well as the defendants in the other school-desegregation cases, Davis and the other opposing attorneys stated that integrating the schools would be bad for white children, whose education would suffer as a result. Thurgood replied the following day:

> I got the feeling on hearing the points made yesterday that when you put a white child in a school with a lot of colored children, the child would fall apart or something. Everybody knows that is not true. These same kids in Virginia and South Carolina—and I have seen them do it—play in the streets together, they play on their farms together, they go down the road together, they come out of school and play ball together. They have to be separated in school. . . . It can't be because of slavery in the past because there are very few groups in this country that haven't had slavery some place back in the history of their groups. It can't be color because there are Negroes as white as the drifted snow, with blue eyes, and they are just as segregated as the colored men. The only thing it can be is an inherent determination that the people who were formerly in slavery, regardless of anything else, shall

be kept as near that stage as possible, and now
is the time, we submit, that this court should
make it clear that that is not what our Constitution stands for.

At another time during his arguments, Thurgood
used the word *equal*. Justice Felix Frankfurter leaned
forward and asked Thurgood exactly what he meant
by *equal*. Thurgood was ready for that question, and
he was ready with a simple, but profound answer.
"Equal," he answered, "means getting the *same* thing,
at the *same* time and in the *same* place."

When the arguments were over, Thurgood felt good
about the case as he had pleaded it. But he realized
that no clear victor had emerged. He had grave doubts
that the Supreme Court would go so far as to outlaw
segregation, and he knew that the nine justices would
deliberate very carefully, probably for months, before
rendering their decision. He turned his attention to
other cases as well as to doing whatever he could to
keep hope alive for downtrodden southern blacks.

Thurgood often traveled to the South to speak to
groups of blacks who were organizing to fight for
their rights. Amzie Moore, a civil rights activist in
Mississippi, recalled how in 1950 he helped organize
blacks in his area "to teach Negroes first-class citizenship": "Our second meeting was in 1952. We brought
in Mr. Marshall, the noted lawyer for the NAACP.
He told us that he had argued before the Supreme
Court about abolishing segregation."

Meanwhile, the nine justices of the Supreme Court had been considering the *Brown* case. Records of private discussions among them indicate that Chief Justice Fred M. Vinson was at first not inclined to rule against segregation. Then, in September 1953, he unexpectedly died of a heart attack. A month later, President Eisenhower nominated Earl Warren to the Court as the new chief justice. That particular combination of events would prove extremely important in the *Brown* case.

Finally, on May 17, 1954, the Court handed down its decision. The justices had voted 9 to 0 in favor of desegregation. Even Thurgood was amazed that the decision had been unanimous. "We must consider public education in the light of its full development and its present place in American life throughout the nation," read the written opinion. "Today, education is perhaps the most important function of state or local governments. . . . Today it is a principal instrument in awakening the child to cultural values, in preparing him for later professional training, and in helping him to adjust normally. . . . We conclude that in the field of public education the doctrine of 'separate but equal' has no place." Chief Justice Warren specifically mentioned the results of Dr. Kenneth Clark's doll test as important in his decision.

After every Supreme Court case that he had won before, Thurgood had celebrated by breaking open a bottle of liquor, announcing, "I'm cooking today," and making everyone his special crab soup. Once, he had danced on the tables of a San Francisco restaurant. Another time, he had decided that all his calls had to go through one of his "seven assistant secretaries," and since he didn't have any assistant secretaries, he immediately deputized his entire office staff as assistant secretaries. But this time, while his friends and colleagues went wild, he was in a curiously subdued and thoughtful mood. He realized that history had been made, that the Court's decision was the most important breakthrough of the twentieth century. It was just too big to celebrate. He found himself thinking about Charles Hamilton Houston and wishing he could have lived to see this day. Many years later, Thurgood said: "A large number of people never heard of Charles Houston . . . [but] when *Brown against Board of Education* was being argued in the Supreme Court . . . there were some two dozen lawyers on the side of the Negroes fighting for their schools. . . . Of those lawyers, only two hadn't been touched by Charlie Houston. That man was the engineer of all of it." As celebration swirled around him, he muttered: "You fools go ahead and have your fun. Be we ain't begun to work yet."

Not only Thurgood but most legal experts realized that the Supreme Court's decision had much wider application than just to schools. If segregation was wrong in education, then it was also wrong in where people lived, where they could sit on buses, where they could get jobs, where they could get medical care, and where they could swim and play baseball. Thurgood wanted to attack these other areas quickly, and he organized a conference of NAACP lawyers in Atlanta, Georgia, to decide how best to pursue that attack. He hoped to have desegregation well under way by September 1955, and many other black leaders shared his optimism.

They underestimated the reaction of white racists. Far from bowing to the tide of change, many states vowed resistance. Some states—such as Delaware, Maryland, West Virginia, and Missouri—started planning for desegregation. But in the Deep South, the resounding cry was "Never!"

In states such as Mississippi, Alabama, and Georgia, racists formed white citizens' councils, which were very much like the Ku Klux Klan but without the white robes and hoods. Their whole purpose was to terrorize any black person who tried to register to vote, tried to get his local school board to desegregate, or in any way tried to exercise his equal rights. They engaged in kidnapping, beating, shooting, and even lynching in the name of protecting the white southern way of life. Unfortunately, these racists soon had an ally in the Supreme Court.

The Court's decision in *Brown v. Board of Education*, in itself, was not enough, for it had made no mention of when and how the states were to go about desegregating the schools. Instead, the Court had ordered reargument, to be held in April 1955, on the question of how to remedy the problem of segregated schools. The Court's main concern was whether de-segregation should be immediate or gradual.

Needless to say, attorneys for the southern states argued for gradual desegregation. Thurgood realized that schools couldn't be integrated overnight. But he worried about what the southern states meant by *gradual.* He made notes about the issue, writing at one point that the state of Maryland had taken sixteen years after the Supreme Court's decision in *Gaines ex rel. Canada v. Missouri* to get around to abolishing its system of out-of-state scholarships for black students. Wrote Thurgood, "Now after all of this shit—no valid reason for delay—no hope that time would help."

His misgivings would prove to be well-founded. The Supreme Court ordered that desegregation was to take place "with all deliberate speed," which was about the most unclear instruction it could have given. To a black parent, *all deliberate speed* meant within a year. To a southern state, it meant twenty-five years or, even better, never. Most southern states continued to believe that the federal government had no business telling them how to run their education systems, and they planned to drag their feet on desegregation as long as they could.

As soon as the Supreme Court handed down its decision, Thurgood—who had gone to Washington, D.C., to await it—grabbed a copy of it and headed for New York. There he and other NAACP national officers sat down and tried to figure out what the

Court meant. They were disappointed that the Court had set no fixed deadline for desegregation. Nevertheless, they agreed that they had to at least act as if they had won. Roy Wilkins, who had recently become executive director after the death of Walter White, called a press conference to say that he and the NAACP thought the Court had acted positively. Thurgood stepped forward to say that he and his legal team were "ready, willing and able" to see that the South obeyed the law. Governor Herman Talmadge of Georgia had responded to the Court's decision by saying that he would personally make sure that none of Georgia's 159 counties followed the Court's ruling. Thurgood responded that if Georgia really tried to do that, he would personally go into every county in the state to make sure that the law was obeyed. One of the reporters who had been invited to the news conference asked him how long the fight might take if the entire South behaved as Georgia was threatening. Thurgood thought for a moment and answered, "It will not take one hundred years—*that* I can guarantee."

Thurgood realized that he and others whose lives were devoted to fighting segregation in the courts had a long road ahead of them. They would have to take many school boards to court to force them to at least begin to desegregate. It would be years before they got anywhere. But he knew he had to keep fighting. "If we stop now, we're lost," he said in 1955. "They're going to try everything in the book to get out from under. Our job is to stay ahead of them."

Then he learned that the woman who had given him so much support over the years would not be around much longer. Buster had cancer.

She had been suffering from the disease for more than a year before Thurgood found out how sick she really was. Her doctor had decided not to be truthful about how long she had to live, fearing that she and Thurgood might give up hope if they knew the truth. Thurgood almost collapsed when he learned of his wife's real condition. He felt angry about not being told. If he'd only known, he would have spent more time with Buster. Now that he did know, he devoted every spare moment to his wife.

All through the fall of 1954 and the winter, Thurgood took personal charge of Buster's care, and in the last six weeks of her illness, he rarely left her side. He wouldn't go out of the apartment and refused to see even his closest friends. Buster died in February 1955, leaving him desolate for a time. "I thought the end of the world had come," he said. "I had no thoughts on remarriage." But it never seriously occurred to Thurgood to give up the fight for equality, and after Buster's funeral, he threw himself into his work, burying his grief in endless days of traveling, giving speeches, and attacking segregation on every legal front he could find.

Within a few months, to his great surprise, he had fallen in love again. Cecilie "Cissy" Suyat was a Hawaiian who had come to the NAACP as a secretary in 1948. Nineteen years younger than Thurgood, and two feet, one inch shorter, she seemed an unlikely woman for Thurgood to love. Indeed, the first time he proposed to her, in August 1955, she declined. But she was calm and serene and, like Buster, able to handle the fact that Thurgood was engaged in important work and often did not have much time for her. When he proposed again, she accepted. They were married in early 1956. Cissy was soon pregnant and quit her job at the NAACP. Thurgood was overjoyed at the prospect of having children, for his one regret about his marriage to Buster was that they had been unable to have children. He and Cissy had two sons, Thurgood, Jr. (also called Goody), born in late 1956, and John, born two years later. Thanks to the efforts of people like their father, Thurgood, Jr. and John would never experience the segregation that he had suffered when he was growing up.

8

The Direct Action Civil Rights Movement Begins

On the evening of December 1, 1955, a black woman named Rosa Parks refused to give up her seat on a Montgomery, Alabama, city bus to a white man. She was arrested for breaking the local segregation laws. She was not the first black person in Montgomery to be arrested for this same "crime," but it was her arrest that finally spurred the black people of Montgomery to action. Community leaders called for a black boycott of the city's buses, and it was highly successful. A group of local black ministers formed the Montgomery Improvement Association (MIA) and elected as president a young minister new to town. His name was Martin Luther King, Jr.

The MIA did not demand an end to all segregation on the buses. All it asked for was seating on a first come, first served basis, with whites sitting from the front to the middle and blacks sitting from the back to the middle. The MIA also asked that blacks no longer have to pay at the front, then go around to the back to board the bus. These were very modest demands. But they were still too much for the whites of Montgomery.

The white authorities and white racist citizens tried every legal means they could to get the blacks back on the buses. When those tactics failed, they turned to violence. At the end of January 1956, the local White Citizens' Council planted bombs at the homes of King and other leaders of the boycott. Thurgood was furious. He declared that the NAACP would defend every boycotter or boycott leader who was arrested. Meanwhile, NAACP branches around the country sent contributions to the MIA. The MIA raised money to buy station wagons to transport black Montgomeryites to and from work. Private citizens volunteered to coordinate the pickups and drop-offs. As the boycott wore on, the buses had to stop running, since the majority of their riders were black. Altogether, Montgomery's blacks stayed off the buses for more than a year and only agreed to return after the city and the bus company promised to honor their demands.

A week after the bombs went off at the homes of Dr. King and other boycott leaders in Montgomery, Thurgood accompanied Autherine Lucy as she registered for the second time at the University of Alabama. A black woman who wanted to become a librarian and who could not find a black school in Alabama that offered a degree in library science, she had first applied to the University of Alabama in 1952 and had been accepted. But when she had arrived on campus and it was discovered she was black, she was not admitted. She had then enrolled in Mills College, a black school in Tuscaloosa.

On graduation from Mills College, she still wanted to be a librarian. So in 1956 she once again attempted to enroll at the university. This time, however, she had the backing of the NAACP.

In the years between 1952 and 1956, the Texas and Oklahoma court cases had been decided in favor of black students, and black students had entered graduate schools in Tennessee, Kentucky, Missouri, North Carolina, Virginia, Delaware, and Arkansas. But Alabama was not going to bow to the federal courts.

On the day Autherine Lucy, who was twenty-six years old, arrived on campus, a mob of young whites threw rocks and eggs at her and cried, "Kill her, kill her." The university did nothing to stop the mob or help her. It also barred her from the university dormitory. After a few weeks, she withdrew. NAACP lawyers took her case to the federal district court in Birmingham, which ordered her reinstated. But the university argued that she had treated the trustees with disrespect and expelled her.

Autherine Lucy was a brave young woman, but by this time she was completely demoralized. Hearing this, Thurgood and Constance Baker Motley, who by now was a practicing attorney with the NAACP, flew to Alabama to take her back to New York. There the NAACP called a press conference in which Lucy said that no matter what had happened to her, she still had faith in her country. She decided not to pursue the case further. That same year she married the Reverend Hugh Foster and later moved to Shreveport, Louisiana, where she taught sixth grade. She never earned the library science degree for which she had gone through so much. The University of Alabama remained segregated until 1963, when two black students successfully integrated it.

In the fall of 1957, the year following the end of the Autherine Lucy case, Thurgood was in Little Rock, Arkansas, where nine black students were trying to integrate Central High School. The school board of Little Rock had announced in 1955 that it would comply with the Supreme Court's 1954 ruling in *Brown v. Board of Education*. But the school board's plan was to go slow and to begin by admitting only a few black students to one white high school, Central High. In February 1956, Wiley Branton, chairman of the NAACP's Legal Redress Committee, filed suit in federal district court hoping to force immediate integration of the Little Rock schools.

When the federal district court judge rejected the suit, Thurgood joined Branton in appealing the case to the U.S. District Court of Appeals for the Eighth District in Saint Louis, Missouri. In April 1957 the court ruled that the school board should allow no further delays in implementing its integration plan. But of the seventy-five black students who applied to Central High, only nine were eventually accepted.

Even they were too many for Governor Orval Faubus, who had promised during his election campaign that he would never allow integration in the state of Arkansas. Just before the opening day of school, he went on local television to announce that he would not be responsible for the violence that would occur if the nine black students entered Central High. He even ordered the National Guard to the school, and when the nine students arrived, they were barred from the door.

Now, the NAACP appealed directly to President Dwight D. Eisenhower, and the president federalized the Arkansas National Guard and ordered them to protect the students. He also sent in one thousand paratroopers to restore order. These actions infuriated the white citizens of Little Rock, who resented outside interference. The issue of states' rights was a major one in the minds of the people of the South, largely because the South had been occupied by federal troops after the Civil War. A mob of whites gathered at the school in screaming protest, threatening bodily harm to the students if they registered.

It was a dangerous time, and no two men were more aware of the danger than Thurgood and Wiley Branton. While in Little Rock, they stayed at the home of Daisy Bates, a local NAACP activist. They shared a large front room with twin beds, and they had signs made up that read "Thurgood Marshall" and "Wiley Branton" to identify the beds. Each tried to put the other's name on the bed closest to the window since that bed was more likely to be bombed. The small joke helped both men to get through the dangerous nights in Little Rock.

The students remained at Central High for a year, although every day was dangerous and degrading for them. The following year, Governor Faubus closed the Little Rock schools entirely. When they reopened in September 1959, they were again segregated.

Partly as a result of Little Rock, Congress passed and President Eisenhower signed the Civil Rights Act of 1957, the first civil rights legislation passed by Congress since the Reconstruction period after the Civil War. It established a Civil Rights Division in the Department of Justice, created a Civil Rights Commission, and empowered the federal government to go to court against anyone who tried to deprive black people of their right to vote. Unfortunately, in order to get the law passed over the vehement opposition of southern congressmen and the concerns of even moderate congressmen, those who supported it had to make many compromises. The law that was passed was much weaker than the one originally proposed. Even so, southerners vowed not to obey it.

A similar thing happened with the next civil rights bill, passed in 1960. Although it was supposed to strengthen the 1957 law, especially regarding voting rights, Thurgood commented, "It would take two or three years for a good lawyer to get someone registered under this bill."

The Deep South was proving to be a tough nut to crack. Thurgood, with his abiding faith in the law, had trouble understanding why other Americans did not share his respect for it.

The ugliness of the Autherine Lucy case and of southern white reactions to other attempts by blacks to gain equality caused some whites to suggest that blacks were pushing too hard. They advised blacks to go slow and give southern whites a chance to get used to the idea of equal rights. But Thurgood brushed aside such advice. "They don't mean go slow," he said, "They mean don't go." But he was not in favor of the kind of mass action that had been used by the Montgomery bus boycotters, even though it had worked in that particular case. He believed that such actions would just make southern white racists more determined than ever to keep segregation alive. He feared that many blacks would lose their lives as a result and believed that violence should be avoided at all costs.

He was especially critical of the idea that nonviolent protest could be used to end school segregation, remarking once that desegregation was men's work and should not be entrusted to children. Like other top executives at the NAACP, he regarded King, who was twenty years younger than he, as an "opportunist," and a "first-rate rabble rouser." He strongly believed that the more responsible, businesslike approach of the NAACP to civil rights would be more successful in the end. Moreover, even if he had felt personally inclined to challenge the segregation that he faced every day he spent in the South, he believed that he had no right to do so as long as he worked for the NAACP. "I ride in the for-colored-only cabs and in the back end of streetcars—quiet as a mouse," he said in 1957. "I eat in Negro cafes and don't use white washrooms. I don't challenge the customs personally, because I figure I'm down South representing a client—the NAACP—and not myself."

Because of his reputation in the legal community and his comparatively moderate stance on the tactics to be used to gain equality for black people, Thurgood Marshall's stature increased in the white community as well. He enjoyed considerable publicity in the white press, especially after the *Brown v. Board of Education* ruling by the Supreme Court. Next to Dr. Ralph Bunche, who helped to establish the United Nations and to address Palestinian issues after Israeli nationhood, and Roy Wilkins, executive director of the NAACP, Thurgood was the most well-known black man in America.

His reputation extended past the borders of the United States. His name was also well known in Europe, and he was particularly popular in Africa, where many former European colonies were gaining their independence in the late 1950s and early 1960s. Because of his international reputation, he was named by President Dwight D. Eisenhower to head the United

States delegation to the Third United Nations Congress in Stockholm, Sweden. In 1960, he was the personal guest of President William V. S. Tubman when Tubman took office in the African nation of Liberia.

In the presidential election of 1960, the candidate of the Democratic Party, John F. Kennedy, won, succeeding the Republican President Eisenhower. Thurgood continued to be a black leader to whom the president of the United States turned to represent him abroad. In 1961, President Kennedy asked him to be his personal representative at the independence ceremonies of the nation of Sierra Leone in Africa.

Thurgood, who had been brought up on stories of the old, feisty African-born slave in his family, was honored to be present at these ceremonies marking the independence of African nations. He was grateful to have lived long enough to see the history of black people in America come full circle: from slaves brought from Africa to America to official representatives from America back to Africa.

He was especially honored when he was asked by the nation of Kenya to attend the 1961 Kenya Constitutional Conference in London and to help Kenya write its new constitution. He took a leave of absence from his work at the NAACP in order to devote the time necessary for this task.

Kenya was a former British colony, and during its years under the British, many whites had moved to Kenya. So had many Asians from British colonies in India and Malaysia. Still, native-born black Kenyans were in the majority. The new constitution had to be written to safeguard the rights of the minority Europeans and Asians who would be living with a black majority. While Thurgood took his assignment very seriously, sometimes he had to laugh at the idea that he, who had spent almost his entire career fighting for the rights of a black minority in a white-majority country was now writing a consitution to safeguard a white minority in a black-majority country. When the new Kenyan constitution was completed, Thurgood understood a lot better the problems of the United States in balancing the rights of its various population groups. The new constitution pleased very few people. The whites and Asians worried that their rights were not sufficiently protected, while the blacks worried that the rights of the minority groups were being too well protected.

On September 23, 1961, not long after he finished helping to write the new Kenyan constitution, Thurgood was named by President Kennedy to a judgeship on the United States Court of Appeals for the Second Circuit, which covered New York, Connecticut, and Vermont. He was only one of a large number of blacks whom Kennedy named to federal posts. His former NAACP colleague, Spottswood Robinson, was named by the president to the Civil Rights Commission. Thurgood's appointment required the approval of Congress, and Thurgood, not to mention the president, realized he faced an uphill fight. Southern congressmen could never forgive him for upsetting the segregated southern way of life.

In hearings on Thurgood's appointment, Senator Olin D. Johnson of South Carolina charged that he was a one-sided lawyer, meaning that his only experience was in civil rights. Other southern senators supported Olin and together managed to tie up consideration of Thurgood's appointment for nearly a year. The Senate adjourned its 1961 session without confirming Thurgood. So President Kennedy appointed him to an interim seat on the court. When Congress convened in January 1962, there were more delays, and it was not until late August 1962 that he was finally confirmed. Northern congressmen rallied to his cause, and when his appointment finally came to a vote in the Senate, it was approved by an almost three-fourths majority.

Other Kennedy appointments of blacks to the federal bench had not been such ordeals. But southerners could not forget Thurgood's starring role in the legal battle to desegregate the schools, and they had let their representatives in Washington, D.C., know it. It was a severe ordeal for Thurgood, but he never criticized the process. "I think protest is part of the American way of life," he said years later. "The right to petition Congress is in the Constitution. So I think any individual or any group has the specific right to present to Congress their views on any matter that is before Congress. The Senate committee held hearings for eleven months before they got around to confirming me, but I still think they had that duty."

Thurgood accepted the appointment with great and honest humility. He thanked his supporters in the Senate and refused to speak ill of those who had tried to prevent him from taking the post. "They really don't hate me as a person," he said of the southern senators, "even though they barked real loud and called me everything but a child of God. They had to watch out for *their* political hides and they did whatever they had to. I'm just a symbol to them—a symbol of something that is destroying their view of the Constitution. Lord help them! Some day they'll see the light."

Being a judge on the court of appeals was a full-time job, and when Thurgood accepted the appointment, he had to give up his position with the NAACP. He had mixed feelings about leaving the organization, for he knew there was still much to be done. He was not the only NAACP lawyer who had left the organization; others had left to take posts in higher education and government. But he, like them, had worked long and hard for the organization. They had trained the younger attorneys well, and they had to have confidence that the younger attorneys for the NAACP could carry on without them.

Their confidence was well placed. Many of the younger NAACP attorneys also were later elected or appointed to government offices. Robert Carter was named a federal district court judge. Constance Baker Motley, who was an intern at the NAACP legal department under Thurgood, went on to become the first and only woman to be elected borough president of Manhattan, and she later became a federal district court judge.

For Thurgood, taking the new job meant taking himself out of the front lines of the civil rights battle. As a judge, he would have to be impartial and not read more into the Constitution than was there. He would also be more stationary, sitting on a bench instead of traveling all around the country to plead cases in local courtrooms. Recalling his time as a judge, his secretary told a reporter for *Life* Magazine: "He never complained about the court. In fact, he said he liked it. But often his only visitor would be the bailiff. The other justices kept their chamber doors closed, but he insisted that his be kept open. We said he did that because he is so nosy—he always wanted to know what was going on."

On the other hand, the job, which paid a comfortable salary, gave him financial security for the first time in his life. Being in one place would also be a nice change. He would get to spend more time with his family, and he looked forward to being a real father to his two sons. He would not have to suffer the physical exhaustion of constant travel to strange places. And most important, he would not have to face the dangers of unfriendly southern towns where citizens and law enforcement officials alike just waited for the chance to do him harm.

In fact, he began to enjoy the prestige of his position.

But he never let it go to his head. Once, he and a colleague were waiting in a long line at a Washington restaurant. "Just watch," said Thurgood. "Now that I'm a federal judge, we'll get treated right." Pretty soon, the headwaiter approached and led the two men to one of the best tables. Thurgood looked at his colleague as if to say, "See?" Then the waiter asked, "And now, Congressman Powell, what would you like to drink?" The waiter thought Thurgood was Adam Clayton Powell, Jr., the powerful black congressman from New York who was the chairman of the House Education Committee. Thurgood laughed and laughed at the joke on himself.

Thurgood was very familiar with the work of the federal court of appeals, for he had taken many cases to it. The court hears evidence in cases that have already been decided in lower courts but whose decisions are questioned by one side or the other. The court also decides whether to accept the appeals in the first place. The decisions of the court of appeals can also be appealed, this time to the U.S. Supreme Court. Every plaintiff or defendant has this right.

A judge on the court of appeals is supposed to have great knowledge of the law, and it is not good for him or her to have opinions overturned by the U.S. Supreme Court.

In his four years as a judge on the court of appeals, Thurgood heard cases of all types. Some related to civil rights, but others related to tax questions, criminal law, civil law, even the law of the sea. He had to study the Constitution and decisions in similar cases that had been previously decided. Sometimes he felt as if he was back in college. He loved the study of law and enjoyed the work. And his wife, Cissy, complained that he was still working too hard. Like the U.S. Supreme Court, the court of appeals consists of several judges, who collectively decide a case and take turns writing the majority opinion. Altogether, Thurgood wrote more than one hundred opinions, and of his majority opinions, not one was reversed by the Supreme Court. Several of his opinions became the law of the land.

Meanwhile, he had the opportunity to watch his sons grow. They both attended Dalton, a private school in Manhattan, and both shared their father's passion for trains and interest in cowboy movies. Every Sunday the family went to the Episcopal Church near their seventeenth-floor apartment in Morningside Gardens on West 123d Street, and at every meal they shared together—breakfast, lunch, and dinner— Thurgood said grace.

9

Above the Fray

hile Thurgood Marshall was sitting on the federal bench, the Direct Action Civil Rights Movement heated up in the South. The civil rights battleground moved from the courts to the streets, and the battle cry was taken up by ordinary people.

The Montgomery Bus Boycott of 1955–56 had sparked the imagination of the American people, especially black Americans. Martin Luther King, Jr., emerged from that successful campaign as an important civil rights leader who wanted to build on the momentum created by the boycott. He and other southern ministers formed the Southern Christian Leadership Conference to work for the civil rights of black people. Its first major campaign took place in 1960, when King called on blacks to begin "mass violation of immoral laws."

Meanwhile, young black people in the South decided that they were tired of waiting for civil rights cases to make their slow, arduous way through court after court. They wanted equal rights immediately. In Greensboro, North Carolina, in February 1960, students at the black North Carolina Agricultural and Technical College took seats at the local Woolworth's luncheonette, which would not serve blacks, and refused to move until they were arrested and taken away by force. This student sit-in was widely covered in the media, and soon students in other areas were sitting in to protest segregation. By the end of the year, many hotels, movie theaters, libraries, supermarkets, and amusement parks had lowered barriers against black people. In April 1960, black students formed the Student Nonviolent Coordinating Committee to engage in protests against segregation.

That same year, Congress passed another civil rights act, which strengthened the 1957 law and provided criminal penalties for bombings, bomb threats, and mob action designed to obstruct court rulings. That same year the U.S. Supreme Court ruled that discrimination in bus-terminal restaurants on interstate bus lines was unconstitutional, and in 1961 black and white riders who were members of an organization called the Congress of Racial Equality (CORE) decided to test whether bus terminals were obeying the law. They went on a series of "Freedom Rides," in which integrated groups rode interstate buses into the

South. White mobs stoned the Freedom Ride buses and beat the riders, black and white.

In 1962 black citizens of Albany, Georgia, tried to desegregate all public facilities. They failed, primarily because of divisions among the groups leading the demonstrations, which included Martin Luther King, Jr's., Southern Christian Leadership Conference and the Student Nonviolent Coordinating Committee. Later that year, James Meredith, a black student armed with a court order and accompanied by federal troops, enrolled at the University of Mississippi. Two people were killed and many injured in the resulting riots.

In the spring of 1963 in Birmingham, Alabama, another attempt was made to desegregate all the public facilities of a Deep South city. This time, King and the leaders of other civil rights groups learned from their mistakes in Albany and worked together. Sheriff Eugene "Bull" Connor ordered his men to use police dogs and fire hoses against the demonstrators, who included young children. But the demonstrators did not fight back. Carried on television nationwide and throughout the world, this violence against nonviolent black people was shocking to outsiders. Eventually, Birmingham's white businessmen, fearful of the bad name the city was getting, arranged for the desegregation of public facilities in the city.

In June 1963, Medgar Evers, Mississippi chairman of the NAACP, was shot and killed in front of his home. Two months later, 250,000 people, of whom sixty thousand were white, marched on Washington, D.C., in support of more civil rights laws. Three weeks later, a black church in Birmingham was bombed, killing four young black girls—Addie Mae Collins, Denise McNair, Carole Robertson, and Cynthia Wesley. The following June, three members of the Student Nonviolent Coordinating Committee—two whites from New York City, Andrew Goodman and Michael Schwerner, and one black from Mississippi, James Chaney, who were in Mississippi to help register blacks to vote—were murdered. In December, the FBI arrested several white men, including the local sheriff and deputy sheriff, on federal charges of conspiracy to violate the civil rights code. But a U.S. commissioner of the Justice Department dismissed the charges as "hearsay." (Thurgood would later be directly involved in this case.)

In July 1964, President Lyndon B. Johnson, who had become president after the November 1963 assassination of President John F. Kennedy, signed the Civil Rights Act of 1964. It was a strong and far-reaching law that guaranteed blacks the right to vote and to have equal access to public accommodations such as hotels, motels, restaurants, and places of amusement. Not long afterward, on July 18, 1964, blacks in Harlem rioted after a white, off-duty police officer shot a fifteen-year-old black youth. One person was killed, eighty-one civilians and thirty-five police were injured, and there was widespread damage and looting. By the end of the summer, similar riots had occurred in Rochester, New York; Jersey City, Elizabeth, and Paterson, New Jersey; Philadelphia, Pennsylvania; and Chicago, Illinois. Civil rights leaders realized that their concentration on legal segregation had caused them to forget discrimination and lack of opportunity that blacks suffered in the North.

Thurgood was not surprised about what was happening in the North. Back in 1957, he had pointed out in an interview with *U.S. News & World Report* that patterns of residence in northern areas made for segregation. There had to be an end to residential segregation in those areas, he said. "There had to be freedom to move.

"Even in the North," he continued, "people are conditioned to believe that the Negro is a second-class citizen, to be considered something different. Once you clean up the situation in the South, the North will be an easy job. But we can't let down the constant pressure on the North. It would be a bad job if the Negro gets his rights in the South and loses them in the North."

Action shifted again to the South in 1965. After attempts by blacks in Selma, Alabama, to demonstrate for voting rights, three thousand were arrested, including Dr. Martin Luther King, Jr., who had just won the 1964 international Nobel Prize for Peace. King then called for a march from Selma to Montgomery. President Johnson sent army troops and deputized the Alabama National Guard to protect the marchers. Nevertheless, a white housewife from Detroit named

Viola Liuzzo, who was transporting marchers to and from the march, was murdered by a carload of Ku Klux Klansmen.

Thurgood followed all these events with great interest and emotion. Sometimes, people suggested that he should be taking part, not just observing. But Thurgood was a federal judge who was supposed to be impartial. He could not get involved. Besides, he had no interest in being involved. When friends suggested that he go to Selma for the march, he responded: "You can't be serious. Why, I was on that road—from Selma to Montgomery—before any of these kids were born and when their parents wouldn't be caught within a mile of it." He had always preferred the battlefield of the courts, and reason told him that the time for him to be on the front lines of the struggle had passed. "I knew I couldn't finish the job," he said, "but I had to get the basic portion done."

Still, he was often sought out for advice, and sometimes he gave it, unofficially. He was alternately overjoyed and dismayed by the turn of events that had taken place in the civil rights movement. Especially at first, he wondered if people like Martin Luther King, Jr., were doing the right thing by challenging the system of segregation in the South by direct action on the streets. He advised continuing to fight the battle in the courts. After all, the keys to equality for black people were present in the Constitution; they just needed enlightened judges to find them. Even if changing the law in the courts took much longer than getting Congress to pass new laws, Thurgood felt that the Constitutional path was the better way. But he had to admire the courage of the common black people who were putting their lives on the line for their rights, and over time he came to agree that direct action was a far quicker way to win laws guaranteeing equality. The Constitution provided for the president and the Congress to make laws, according to the will of the people. The nonviolence of the demonstrators had touched the hearts of many white Americans, and the violence of southern white racists had turned their stomachs. The president of the United States, and the Congress of the United States had responded to the will of the people.

The president who proposed and signed into law more civil rights legislation than any other twentieth-century president before or since, was a southerner. Born and raised in Texas, Lyndon Baines Johnson had spent many years in Congress and had watched the ebb and flow of the political tide. He knew how to get things done in Congress because he was clever at playing the political game that curried and gave favors and traded influence. When he succeeded John F. Kennedy to the presidency, he vowed to press the late president's civil rights agenda. But he wound up pushing through more civil rights than probably even Kennedy had intended.

The strongest, and the last, major civil rights bills were passed during the Johnson presidency. Following the Civil Rights Act of 1964 came the Voting Rights

Act of 1965, and finally, the Civil Rights Act of 1967, which had an open-housing provision.

Also important were President Johnson's appointments of blacks to many federal jobs, including Thurgood Marshall as the first black solicitor general.

The solicitor general is sometimes called the tenth member of the U.S. Supreme Court. The government is a party in more than half the cases the Court hears, and since the solicitor general is the government's chief appellate lawyer, the Court sees, hears, and pays attention to him more than to any other man. He is not only the government's lawyer but the Court's lawyer as well, for part of his job is to decide which cases should go to the Supreme Court. The Court relies on him greatly to block appeals that are not worthy of the Court's time. And because the solicitor general is supposed to be objective, the Court usually accepts the appeals that he does bring to it.

The solicitor general is not someone who makes the news much, even though he is the third-ranking member of the Justice Department, behind the attorney general and his deputy. The job is a tough one, for many appeals come to his desk, and he must study each one thoroughly in order to accept or reject it. Once he accepts an appeal, he and his staff often rewrite it totally. After that, he represents the government in oral arguments before the Supreme Court.

One day in July 1965, Thurgood was interrupted in a private dining room in the federal courthouse in Manhattan by a telephone call from the president of the United States. When he took the telephone, the first thing he heard was, "Judge, what does security mean to you?" Thurgood replied: "Mr. President, to a man like me, security means just about everything, I guess. I've worked for security all my life, and it hasn't been an easy thing." Then the president offered him the job of solicitor general. He would replace Archibald Cox, who was retiring from the position to teach at Harvard University.

As solicitor general, Thurgood would again have the opportunity to fight for civil rights, which certainly appealed to him after years of not being able to be a legal activist. But at first, he wasn't at all sure that he wanted to take the new job. For one thing, it paid about $4,500 less per year than the $33,000 a year he was getting as a judge. For another, his judgeship was for life; the solicitor general could expect to be in office only as long as the president who appointed him. Johnson knew that these were major considerations for Thurgood, which is why he got right to the point about security. But Lyndon Johnson was a very persuasive man, and Thurgood later said that by the time the conversation ended, "I was ashamed that I hadn't volunteered. LBJ is a convincing gentleman."

On a more serious note, Thurgood said: "Negroes have made great advances in government and I think it's time they started making some sacrifices. I accepted because the President of the United States asked and, secondly, the President who asked was Lyndon Johnson, who has demonstrated his leadership in civil rights. When he asked you to be a part of what he is doing to give full equality to Negroes, the least you can do is help."

This time confirmation did not take nearly as long. While there was a great hue and cry from southerners when the president announced the appointment on July 13, 1965, Thurgood was voted in by Congress on August 11 and sworn in on August 24.

At the swearing-in ceremony, President Johnson said, "Thurgood Marshall symbolizes what is best about our American society: the belief that human rights must be satisfied through the orderly process of law." Thurgood, an old warhorse, was moved in spite of himself. There, with Cissy, Thurgood, Jr., and John looking on, he was making history as the first black solicitor general.

Supreme Court Justice Hugo Black gave the oath of office to the thirty-third solicitor general in the history of the United States. It was ironic, because Black, a former senator from Alabama, had once been a member of the Ku Klux Klan. Now, he was one of the most liberal members of the Court. "He has good policy judgement and the power of self-control," said Black of Marshall that day. "I know he will do a fine job." Equally ironic was the fact that Thurgood now had the same job as one of the toughest opponents he had ever faced in court—the late John W. Davis, who as solicitor general had argued against Thurgood in the *Brown v. Board of Education* case.

Almost as soon as Thurgood's appointment had

been announced, some people had begun to speculate that Lyndon Johnson really intended to appoint Thurgood as the first black justice of the Supreme Court. Thurgood tried to put that speculation to rest: "I can tell you the President made no promises, there were no deals, there was no talk of it. He wanted me for Solicitor General. That's all."

But an unnamed source who knew both Johnson and Marshall told a reporter for the *New York Times*: "Thurgood's not putting you on. The President wouldn't say anything to him about the Supreme Court. But the point is he doesn't have to. Thurgood knows . . . well that Johnson wants to put Negroes in positions on all levels of government, and he knows this would not by any means exclude the Supreme Court. You're dealing with two wise and canny customers and an awful lot can go unspoken. My bet is he's being set up for the Court. And my bet is he knows it."

Other observers noted that at the swearing-in ceremony at the White House, the president, in what may or may not have been a slip of the tongue, called Thurgood "Justice Marshall."

Thurgood was too busy relocating to Washington, D.C., to speculate about his future. He took a small apartment until the family could join him a month or so later. There was the flurry of finding a house in the integrated Capital Park section of southwest Washington, moving in, and getting the boys registered at Georgetown Day School, a private school in Georgetown, part of Washington where they now lived. Meanwhile, he was settling into his new routine and learning his new responsibilities.

On October 14, when it opened its fall term, Thurgood was formally presented to the Supreme Court. It was traditional for the solicitor general to wear formal dress when presented to the Court, including striped pants, a vest, and a morning coat (a cutaway, or swallow-tail, jacket). No one saw any reason to change this ritual. Many men would have had to go out and buy or rent such an outfit, but Thurgood just happened to have one. Back in 1960, when he had been President Eisenhower's representative to the inauguration of President Tubman of Liberia, he had bought just such a tuxedo. He only had to take it out of mothballs for his formal presentation to the Supreme Court. "Now isn't this the silliest get-up in the world?" he joked as he set off for the Court. But in reality, he didn't feel at all strange in the outfit, for it seemed to fit in at the velvet-draped, marble chambers of the Court. He beamed when Chief Justice Earl Warren said, "The Court welcomes you."

Thurgood realized he had a lot to learn, and he retained the staff that Archibald Cox left behind. The staff included experts in many areas of the law in which he felt he needed help, and he planned to let them handle the cases at which they would be best. He would take on the cases where he felt he could be most effective—civil rights cases.

By the time Thurgood became solicitor general, the

major civil rights legislation had already been passed. Now, court cases in civil rights had to do with refining and interpreting the laws. Thurgood was especially interested in cases involving whether the government could prosecute whites in the South accused of killing blacks: If such murders were ruled civil rights crimes, then the government could prosecute the accused under the civil rights laws; but if they were ruled ordinary crimes, then the states had the responsibility of prosecuting. He was also interested in what he called the "confession question": whether a defendant's confession was admissible in court if it was given without the presence of a lawyer for the defendant.

At the Supreme Court, Thurgood argued that the government should be allowed to bring federal criminal charges against the killers of the three young men who had been lynched in Philadelphia, Mississippi, in 1964. Thurgood's task was to prove that the crime was racially motivated—that the young men had been killed specifically because they were working for black voting rights—and thus that the killers could be tried in the federal courts. He won that case, and in October 1967, after a new trial, an all-white federal court jury convicted seven men on charges of conspiracy to murder. The convicted men included the deputy sheriff and the imperial wizard of the local Ku Klux Klan. It was the first time in the history of the state that whites had been convicted for a crime against blacks.

In another case, Thurgood argued for the right of individual privacy against the FBI, a branch of the same Justice Department in which he himself served. The FBI had been planting listening devices in private homes and offices, sometimes spying on innocent people. Thurgood argued that private citizens needed greater protection from such government spying and proved that in more than twenty cases the Justice Department had used listening devices illegally. The Court ruled that the FBI had acted against the law.

Thurgood worked and studied hard as solicitor general. He successfully argued fourteen of nineteen Supreme Court cases for the government. And of these cases, several were in the areas of antitrust and labor, areas in which he'd had no previous background. But this job was one of the briefest of his career in the law. On June 13, 1967, less than two years after he was appointed solicitor general, President Johnson appointed him as the first black justice on the U.S. Supreme Court.

10

Mr. Justice Marshall

On October 2, 1967, Thurgood Marshall placed his hand on the Bible and promised "to administer justice without respect to persons, and to do equal right to the poor and to the rich ... according to the best of my abilities and understanding." Then he walked up to the long bench of the Supreme Court of the United States and took his seat behind it. He was fifty-nine years old, and he had just become the first black associate justice on the highest court in the land.

Now, he was a member of the very court that had made the most important decisions in civil rights law in a century, and he had been appointed by the U.S. president who had signed into law more civil rights bills than any other president in history, Lyndon B. Johnson.

An opening on the Supreme Court had occurred

when sixty-seven-year-old Justice Tom Clark had decided to retire after eighteen years on the nation's highest bench. Although he was in good health, he did not want to run into any problems of conflict of interest, because his son, Ramsey, had just been named attorney general by President Johnson. Johnson had appointed Ramsey Clark, a fellow Texan, because he felt that Clark could do the job of attorney general, not because he expected Clark's father to vacate his seat on the Supreme Court. However, the vacant seat gave him the opportunity he had been waiting for: to make history by appointing the first black associate justice.

In doing so, he brought the complexion of the Court another step along. Traditionally white, male, and Protestant (although it had welcomed its first Jewish member, Louis D. Brandeis, in 1916), the Court now had its first black member. It would take another fourteen years before the first woman took her seat on the Supreme Court.

In announcing the appointment of Thurgood as the newest associate justice, President Johnson made no direct mention of race. What he did say that sunny afternoon in the White House Rose Garden was this: "I believe that Thurgood Marshall has already earned his place in history, but I think it will be greatly [advanced] by his service on the Court. He is best qualified by training and by very valuable service to the country. I believe it is the right thing to do, the right time to do it, the right man and the right place."

Reaction to the appointment was predictable. Liberals and civil rights activitists hailed it. Southerners criticized it. At the confirmation hearings in the Senate, southern senators subjected Thurgood to a barrage of questions about his competency to serve on the highest court in the land.

"Mr. Solicitor General, isn't it true that you were responsible for getting the Supreme Court to favor our criminals by restricting the use of voluntary confessions?" asked one senator.

"Sir, I once represented an Oklahoma man who 'voluntarily' confessed after he was banged on and beaten up for three days," replied Thurgood, recalling the case of W. D. Lyons a quarter of a century earlier.

Remarked another senator: "Some of your views, Mr. Solicitor General, label you clearly as a liberal to the core. Your addition to the Court would throw it completely off keel, with disastrous results for the nation."

Thurgood responded: "May I observe, sir, that your estimate of my importance is extremely flattering. If I believed that my views in a given case would affect my giving a just decision, I would disqualify myself!"

In the end, the Senate confirmed Thurgood's appointment by a vote of 69 to 11. Even a few southerners voted with the majority, perhaps agreeing with the president that it was "the right time." Thurgood's confirmation as an associate justice on the Supreme Court took no time at all compared to the same process leading to his judgeship on the U.S. Court of

Appeals for the Second Circuit, which was an indication of how far the nation's thinking had come in only six years.

Thurgood was fifty-nine years old when he joined the Supreme Court. He could expect ten to fifteen years on the bench, according to an editorial in *National Review*. But since Supreme Court justices are appointed for life, the number of years he would serve depended very much on his health and on his attitude toward retirement. He joined a Supreme Court that was known for its liberal interpretations of the Constitution. Usually on the conservative side were Justices Hugo Black, Byron White, and Potter Stewart. Usually on the liberal side were Chief Justice Earl Warren, William Brennan, William O. Douglas, Abe Fortas, and John M. Harlan. Justice Tom Clark, whose seat Thurgood was taking over, had usually voted with the conservatives. Many observers expected the more liberal Thurgood to tip the balance even more to the liberal side.

During his first term on the Court, Thurgood did very little tipping. In fact, by the end of March 1968, he had disqualified himself from forty out of the fifty-four cases decided after argument. The reason was that he had dealt with those cases as solicitor general and felt it would be a conflict of interest if he now ruled on them as a Supreme Court justice.

It was an unusual circumstance, but not unheard of. One other justice in recent times had gone to the Court from the solicitor general's position. Justice

Stanley Forman Reed, then retired, stated that he had done the same thing and that "Justice Marshall's action is perfectly in keeping with practice." But with the Court's load at an all-time high, all the justices looked forward to the time when the cases that Thurgood had handled as solicitor general would be taken care of, leaving him free at last to participate in the Court's decisions. By Thurgood's third session on the Court, he was participating in almost all the decisions.

During his first two sessions, Thurgood took on more than the usual number of petitions that ask the Court to hear a case. He worked most Saturdays and even some Sundays. In this way, he could make up for not being able to participate in more of the decisions. He did not mind doing this work. For a man who as a child had spent afternoons in the school basement reading the Constitution as punishment, and his adult life trying to persuade various courts that the Constitution should include all Americans, the chance to interpret that document was a dream fulfilled.

Each justice has several law clerks, who often do the research and even write the opinions of the justices. Thurgood chose highly intelligent clerks and trusted them to do their jobs well. He hired women clerks, which not all the other justices did. He loved to regale his clerks with stories of the days when he was with the NAACP, and when they pleaded that they had work to do, he would go and visit the clerks who worked for other justices. He got along well at the Court; unlike some other new justices, he did not feel insecure about his right to be there. He felt he had every right and was very confident—even in the early days when the justices got together in conference to discuss cases—that he could be effective as a moral force on the Court.

According to Bob Woodward and Scott Armstrong, who wrote a book about the inner workings of the Supreme Court called *The Brethren*: "Marshall had not sought and had not wanted the appointment. He preferred the more active give-and-take of public-interest law. His jurisprudence [knowledge of the law] was long settled; so at conference, Marshall was relaxed, almost intuitively reaching his common-sense solution. He had fit easily into the Warren liberal majority. Plain-spoken and direct, Marshall saw his job as casting his vote and urging his colleagues to do what was right."

During the beginning of the 1969 session of the Court, a case came up on an issue that should have been settled fifteen years earlier, when the Court had ruled in the *Brown v. Board of Education* case. It was a suit filed by the NAACP against delay of desegregation in thirty-three Mississippi school districts. The main question was, what had the 1954 Court meant by "all deliberate speed"? Many southern school districts had used all kinds of evasive tactics to fight desegregation. The NAACP wanted the Court to stop these delays. In discussions of the case *Alexander v. Holmes County Board of Education*, Thurgood argued strongly that the Court must do so. In the end, the Court ruled that "all deliberate speed" was "no longer Constitutionally permissible" and that no delay would be permitted. The Court was unanimous in its decision.

During his time on the Supreme Court, Thurgood was involved in rulings in many memorable cases. One of the most famous was a case that became known as the Pentagon Papers case. The Court held that the American press had a right to free speech, even when that right included printing secret government documents, which in this particular case showed that the government had lied to the American people about the Vietnam War for three decades. Thurgood voted with the majority in this 1971 case.

Another famous case was the 1973 *Roe v. Wade*, in which, broadly interpreted, the Court held that it was a woman's constitutional right to have an abortion. Thurgood voted with the majority in this case, too. Still another was *Regents of the University of California v. Bakke*, over whether racial quotas for minorities in admissions programs were constitutional. Allan Bakke, a white man, had charged that he was unfairly denied admission to the university because he was white. The Court handed down a two-part decision in this case. In one part, the majority ruled that the quotas were unconstitutional; Thurgood dissented. In the second part, Thurgood was in the majority, which said that race could be considered as one of many factors in admitting students.

There were many cases that were not as famous. In

general, Thurgood could be counted on to vote for the rights of privacy, free speech, and protection from unfair treatment by law enforcement authorities, and against the death penalty and any kind of race or sex discrimination.

Although the justices try to be objective, the way they interpret the Constitution does depend a great deal on their personal viewpoints, and it was not long before the balance on the Court began to tip the opposite way. Chief Justice Earl Warren retired two years after Thurgood arrived, and Associate Justice Abe Fortas resigned after it was revealed that he had accepted payments from a corporation while a district judge. This gave Republican Richard M. Nixon—who had been elected president in 1968 after President Johnson had chosen not to run again—two vacancies on the court to fill. He chose men who held more conservative views, the new chief justice, Warren E. Burger, and Associate Justice Harry Blackmun. In 1971, two more vacancies occurred, and Nixon named Lewis F. Powell and William H. Rehnquist to take their places. These men, too, were conservatives. Still, it was this Court that voted 7 to 2 in the famous *Roe v. Wade* abortion case. Three Nixon appointees voted with the majority. The opinion was handed down on Monday, January 22, 1973, the day that former President Johnson died.

Having made four appointments to the Supreme Court, President Nixon had already had a greater impact on the Court than most presidents. But apparently he still didn't think that was enough. When Thurgood came down with pneumonia and had to be hospitalized at Bethesda Naval Hospital in Maryland, the president inquired about his condition. Thurgood suspected that Nixon was not so much interested in his health as in whether there would soon be another vacancy on the Court—Thurgood's seat. He told a navy officer, "Well, Admiral, you have my permission to give it [a condition report] to him only on one condition: that you put at the bottom of it, quote, 'Not Yet.'"

After President Nixon was forced to resign over the Watergate scandal and Vice President Gerald R. Ford became president, Associate Justice William O. Douglas retired. Ford nominated another conservative.

During the four years that Democratic President Jimmy Carter occupied the White House, no justices retired, and so he had no opportunity to name a justice to the Supreme Court. If he'd had that chance, he most certainly would have nominated a liberal. If he'd been able to retain the presidency a second term, he would have had that chance. But he was voted out of office.

Stephen L. Carter, a professor of law at Yale University, was a clerk for Thurgood during the 1980–81 term. A month into that term, in early November 1980, Republican candidate Ronald Reagan defeated Jimmy Carter in a landslide victory. According to Stephen Carter, the next morning, as Thurgood was on his way to the robing room, he met Associate Justice

William Brennan, who looked as if he might have tears in his eyes:

"Mr. Marshall, towering over his friend, looked down, hesitated, then slipped his arm around Mr. Brennan's narrow shoulders. They walked to the robing room that way, passing in and out of the shadows where the brilliant morning sunlight struck curtains or walls. That is the moment when the era ended, as these two great soldiers of liberalism squared their shoulders and marched off to fight their battle against the new political order."

During President Ronald Reagan's two terms in office, he named three justices, including the first woman associate justice, Sandra Day O'Connor. All were known for their conservative views.

The Supreme Court has a tradition of great secrecy. Justices do not as a rule give interviews, and it is an unwritten rule that no one divulges the deliberations in a case before a decision is rendered. Thus, Thurgood did not say publicly how he felt about the number of conservatives on the Court and the way they voted. But he must have found it more and more difficult to serve on the Supreme Court as the viewpoint of the majority of other justices diverged increasingly from his own and that of William Brennan, the other liberal associate justice. On the Supreme Court, the majority rules, and the best Marshall and Brennan could do was write dissenting opinions to the decisions handed down by the majority. It is probably no coincidence that on July 2, 1976, when the Court handed down its decisions in several cases involving the death penalty—decisions that upheld the death penalty in all but one case—Thurgood delivered an angry, emotional dissent, and then went home and had a mild heart attack.

Thurgood would make other angry dissents from the opinions of the conservative majority in the 1980s, for sometimes it seemed to him that they were undoing all the good that the Court had done in the 1950s, 1960s, and 1970s. In February and June 1989, the Court ruled in two important employment discrimination cases. In the first, the Court ruled invalid a Richmond, Virginia, program that set aside portions of public works contracting for minorities. In the second, *Wards Cove Packing v. Antonio*, the Court ruled that employees who charged discrimination had to prove that practices by their employers that were in effect discriminatory were also unnecessary. This meant that it would be much harder for minorities and women to win discrimination suits against their employers.

Although Thurgood must have despaired about the way the Court had shifted to the conservative side, he made no public condemnation of his fellow justices. It was an unwritten rule on the Court that justices did not talk about either the workings of the Court or about their peers, and Thurgood felt honor-bound to keep his thoughts to himself. Besides, his belief in the American system of law was total. There was also an unwritten law that Supreme Court justices did not talk about politics, but this was one rule that Thurgood felt he had to break.

During the late 1980s, the administration of President Ronald Reagan seemed to single out the Supreme Court for criticism. In 1987, the bicentennial of the Constitution, Attorney General Edwin Meese made a series of public statements charging that the Court had often betrayed the "original intent" of the framers of the Constitution. Such statements made Thurgood furious. Meanwhile, as the nation prepared to celebrate the bicentennial of the Constitution, it seemed to Thurgood that all the concentration was being placed on the original document, not on the way it had been interpreted over the years.

In May 1987, Thurgood gave a speech at the annual seminar of the San Francisco Patent and Trademark Law Association, in Maui, Hawaii. In that speech, he said of the Constitution: "I do not believe that the meaning of the Constitution was forever 'fixed' at the Philadelphia Convention. Nor do I find the wisdom, foresight and sense of justice exhibited by the Framers particularly profound. To the contrary, the government they devised was defective from the start, requiring several amendments, a civil war and momentous social transformation to attain the system of constitutional government, and its respect for the individual freedoms and human rights, we hold as fundamental today."

He reminded his audience that when the Framers of the Constitution wrote "We the People," they were not talking about the majority of America's citizens—men who did not own property, women, and blacks. He spoke of how the Founding Fathers had compromised on the question of slavery—New England states had let southern states have slavery, and in exchange the southern states had let the New England states have their way in creating a strong federal government that could regulate commerce. He spoke of how long it had taken Americans to guarantee equality for blacks. "The effects of the Framers' compromises had remained for generations. They arose from the contradiction between guaranteeing liberty and justice to all, and denying both to Negroes."

He said that if citizens sought a "sensitive understanding of the Constitution's inherent defects, and its promising evolution through 200 years of history, the celebration of the 'Miracle at Philadelphia' will, in my view, be a far more meaningful and humbling experience."

He continued:

> We will see that the true miracle was not the birth of the Constitution but its life, a life nurtured through two turbulent centuries of our own making, and a life embodying much good fortune that was not. Thus, in this bicentennial year, we may not all participate in the festivities with flag-waving fervor. Some may more quietly commemorate the suffering, struggle and sacrifice that has triumphed over much of what was

wrong with the original document, and observe the anniversary with hopes not realized and promises not fulfilled. I plan to celebrate the bicentennial of the Constitution as a living document, including the Bill of Rights and other amendments protecting individual freedoms and human rights.

It was the most negative note yet sounded about the celebration of the bicentennial of the Constitution by so prominent a public figure. Thurgood was applauded by some, criticized by many. But he was not about to be silenced. That fall, he broke tradition by granting a television interview to a Chicago columnist named Carl Rowan. Broadcast on public television stations, it was the first formal news interview he had given since President Johnson had appointed him to the Supreme Court. In that interview, he repeated much of what he had said in the speech in Hawaii earlier in the year. He also gave his opinion of President Ronald Reagan, whom he said he placed "at the bottom" among presidents in terms of the rights of blacks. No sitting member of the Supreme Court in recent memory had publicly criticized a sitting president in comments off the bench.

He did not have kind words for many other presidents either, except for Truman and Johnson. With considerable impatience, he said: "I don't know of any president who ever came out, four-square, for ending all segregation in all places. I think it would be good for a president to say, 'People are all people. Take the skin off, there's no difference.' I think it would be good to say so."

Blacks still did not enjoy equal rights, he said, explaining:

> You know, everybody quotes Martin Luther King as saying, 'Thank God, we're free at last.' We're not free, we're nowhere near free. Years ago a Pullman porter told me that he'd been in every state and every city in the country and he'd never been anyplace in this country where he had put his hand up and felt his face to know that he was a Negro. I agree with him. Segregation in general, we still have it. I know that there are clubs here in this town that invite everybody else but me. I don't have an honorary membership in any club in any place under any circumstances.

Asked about his feelings on "original intent," about which Attorney General Edwin Meese had been speaking so often, Thurgood said: "I wish somebody who believes that would ask me what did the Framers mean in the Constitution that would apply to rockets. If you'll tell me what there is in the Constitution that applied to rockets, then I'd understand it. Or wire-tapping. I don't think they had wire-tapping. They barely had wire. The Constitution has to meet the different needs of a different society, and it's there if you look for it."

But, he pointed out, that was the beauty of the document: "I think it's the greatest body of laws ever, and what to me and to many people is so extraordinary about it is that in this late day you find that it works, and when you dig down into it, I don't know of any better job that could have been done. . . . If you read it with any understanding, there's hardly anything that it doesn't cover. It's unbelievable that a constitution written in the horse and buggy days would cover outer space."

Reaction to the interview was highly critical, but Thurgood refused to back down on anything that he had said. In fact, he appeared to be enjoying all the fuss. He had been in poor health for some time. In the summer of 1987, he had been hospitalized for a potentially dangerous blood clot in his foot. Long years of smoking had produced breathing problems, as had long years of being overweight. But in October 1987 he told a conference of lawyers and judges that he had no intention of retiring, even though he knew some of his critics wished he would. He vowed to stay on the Court until he died.

During the next four years the Court continued to change. In a personal loss for Thurgood, his old friend Associate Justice William J. Brennan retired. Former Vice President George Bush, who had succeeded Ronald Reagan as president, named David H. Souter, a conservative judge, to his seat on the Court. With a solidly conservative majority, the Court proceeded to undo much of what Thurgood had worked so hard to create. More and more he found himself as a lonely dissenting voice in decisions affecting private and civil rights.

In the meantime, his health was worsening, and it was probably a combination of poor health and frustration that led him to change his mind about staying on the Supreme Court until he died. In late June 1991, he announced that he would retire as soon as a successor could be named.

In a press conference soon after his announcement, Thurgood insisted that the only reason he was stepping down was ill health and that the decision to retire had been made by him, his wife Cissy, and his doctor: "My doctor, my wife and I have been discussing this for the past six months or more," he said. "And we all eventually agreed, all three of us, that this was it—and this is it."

"What's wrong with you, sir?" asked one of the reporters.

"What's wrong with me?" Thurgood repeated. "I'm old. I'm getting old and falling apart."

Other answers proved that he had not lost his sense of humor or his no-nonsense attitude. Asked about what he planned to do in retirement, he answered, "Sit on my rear end."

There had been reports that he was discouraged about the Court and frustrated and angered by his role as "permanent opposition voice" on it. But he called such reports "a double-barreled lie" and refused to criticize either the Court or the Republican administrations that had nominated so many conservatives to it.

"Everything has to come to an end sometime," he said. "And I have given 50 years to it and if that is not enough, God bless 'em ... President Roosevelt and Churchill died and the world went right along."

Later that summer Thurgood was hospitalized after complaining of lightheadedness. There was no question that his physical condition made retirement a logical move.

Despite his ill health, Thurgood continued to perform his duties as an associate justice while President Bush nominated Clarence Thomas, a judge on the federal court of appeals, and a black man, to take his place. Senate Judiciary Committee confirmation hearings on Thomas's nomination were in progress when attorneys for Warren McCleskey, on death row in a Georgia prison, tried last-minute appeals to the Supreme Court to prevent his execution.

McCleskey was on death row for a conviction in an attempted robbery in 1978. He had admitted to being one of four men involved in the robbery, in which a police officer was killed, but he denied being the one who had shot the officer. None of the other men received the death sentence. He had filed repeated appeals over thirteen years. His last-minute appeal came as a result of the statements of two of his trial jurors, who said that information improperly withheld from them had tainted their decision and that they no longer supported McCleskey's execution.

The Court was not in formal session at that time, but in such cases the justices are polled by telephone. They voted 6 to 3 not to grant McCleskey's appeal. Thurgood dissented from the majority opinion, and later wrote: "In refusing to grant a stay to review fully McCleskey's claims, the Court values expediency over human life. Repeatedly denying Warren McCleskey his constitutional rights is unacceptable. Executing him is inexcusable."

Warren McCleskey was executed. Thurgood Marshall's vote to stay his execution turned out to be the last vote he would cast as a Supreme Court justice. Just days later he announced that he would not join the other associate justices for the start of the 1991–92 Supreme Court session. He was going to retire even before his successor was confirmed.

Thus, on the third Monday in October 1991, as eight black-robed justices took their seats, the chair that Thurgood Marshall had occupied for twenty-four years was empty. Allegations about the personal conduct of Clarence Thomas, whom President Bush had named as Marshall's successor, had forced additional hearings by the Senate Judiciary Committee. There was real doubt that Thomas would be confirmed, though he eventually did take his place on the Supreme Court bench. Thurgood watched the unfolding drama from the sidelines, an elderly, tired, ailing man who had at last given up the fight.

Thurgood Marshall had spent his entire adult life fighting for civil rights and human rights. He'd gone from an "office" in his beat-up 1929 Ford to a seat on the bench of the highest court in the land. He'd fought for black people when they could not drink out of the same water fountain as whites, and he had continued to fight for all people who were discriminated against. Now the fighting was over. He wanted to spend whatever time he had left with his wife of thirty-six years, his sons, and their families. He wanted to read something besides legal briefs. He wanted to write letters, not dissenting opinions.

Many, if not most, men in positions such as Thurgood's write their autobiographies after they retire. In that way, they have some influence over the way history views them. But Thurgood had no intention of writing his memoirs. Then how did he wish to be remembered? he was asked. He answered simply, "He did the best he could with what he had."

Bibliography

Books

Adams, John A., and Joan Martin Burke. *Civil Rights: A Current Guide to the People, Organizations, and Events.* New York: R. R. Bowker, 1970.

Barnes, Catherina A. *Journey from Jim Crow: The Desegregation of Southern Transit.* New York: Columbia University Press, 1983.

Branch, Taylor. *Parting the Waters: America in the King Years 1954–63.* New York: Simon & Schuster, 1988.

Fenderson, Lewis H. *Thurgood Marshall: Fighter for Justice.* New York: McGraw-Hill, 1969.

Forman, James. *The Making of Black Revolutionaries.* New York: Macmillan, 1972.

Huckaby, Elizabeth. *Crisis at Central High: Little Rock 1957–58.* Baton Rouge: Louisiana State University Press, 1980.

Joseph, Joel D. *Black Mondays: Worst Decisions of the Supreme Court.* Bethesda, Md.: National Press, 1987.

Kluger, Richard. *Simple Justice.* New York: Alfred A. Knopf, 1976.

McKissack, Patricia, and Fredrick McKissack. *The Civil Rights Movement in America from 1865 to the Present.* Chicago: Children's Press, 1987.

Parker, Robert. *Capitol Hill in Black and White.* New York: Dodd, Mead & Company, 1986.

Rampersad, Arnold. *The Life of Langston Hughes. Vol. 1, 1902–1941; I, Too, Sing America.* New York: Oxford University Press, 1986.

Tushnet, Mark V. *The NAACP's Legal Strategy Against Segregated Education, 1925–1950.* Chapel Hill: University of North Carolina Press, 1987.

Wilkins, Roy, with Tom Matthews. *Standing Fast: The Autobiography of Roy Wilkins.* New York: Viking, 1982.

Williams, Juan A., ed. *Eyes on the Prize: America's Civil Rights Years, 1954–1965.* New York: Viking, 1987.

Woodward, Bob, and Scott Armstrong. *The Brethren: Inside the Supreme Court.* New York: Simon & Schuster, 1979.

Articles

Allen, Oliver. "Chief Counsel for Equality." *Life,* June 13, 1955, pp. 141–42.

Carter, Stephen L. "An Old Soldier of Liberalism Musters Out." *Wall Street Journal,* July 1, 1991.

"Disqualified." *Time,* Apr. 5, 1968, p. 8.

Gibbs, Nancy. "Filling a Legal Giant's Shoes." *Time,* July 8, 1991, pp. 22–25.

"A Good Court Gets Better." *Christian Century,* June 28, 1967.

Green, Charles. "Marshall to Leave Court: Veteran Justice

Was Its First, Only Black." *Tampa Tribune*, June 28, 1991, pp. 1+.

Labaton, Stephen. "Justice Marshall Vows to Outlive His Critics." *New York Times*, Oct. 18, 1987, p. 33.

Lacayo, Richard. "Right Face!" *Time*, July 1, 1991, pp. 20–23.

"Man in the Middle." *Newsweek*, Sept. 3, 1962, p. 15.

Marable, Manning. "Thurgood Marshall: The Continuing Struggle for Equality." *Black Collegian*, January/February 1990, pp. 72–77.

Molotsky, Irvin. "Slavery Issue Adds Vigor to Debate." *New York Times*, May 21, 1987, p. 1.

"Mr. Justice Marshall." *Newsweek*, June 26, 1967, pp. 34–36.

"Negro Justice." *Time*, June 23, 1967.

"Negro Strategist Sees South on the Run." *U.S. News & World Report*, Sept. 27, 1957, pp. 64–66.

Pierce, Ponchitta. "The Solicitor General." *Ebony*, November 1965, pp. 67–69.

"Portrait of a Leader." *Negro History Bulletin*, November 1955, pp. 26–27.

Rosenthal, Andrew. "Marshall Retires from High Court; Blow to Liberals." *New York Times*, June 28, 1991, pp. 1+.

"A Single-Minded Dual Personality." *Life*, Nov. 12, 1965, pp. 57–58.

"Segregation at the Bar." *Commonweal*, December 25, 1953, p. 296.

Taylor, Stuart, Jr. "Marshall Puts Reagan at 'Bottom' Among Presidents on Civil Rights." *New York Times*, Sept. 9, 1987, p. 1.

———. "Marshall Sounds Critical Note on Bicentennial." *New York Times*, May 7, 1987, p. 1.

"The Tension of Change." *Time*, Sept. 19, 1955, pp. 23–24.

"The Tenth Member." *Time*, Oct. 22, 1965, p. 94.

"Thurgood Marshall Takes a New 'Tush-Tush' Job." *New York Times Magazine*, Aug. 22, 1965, pp. 11+.

"Thurgood Marshall's Honeymoon." *Ebony*, April 1956, pp. 39–45.

"Up from Slavery." *Newsweek*, Oct. 18, 1965, p. 41.

"What the Negro Wants Now." *Ebony*, March 1958, pp. 66–72.

"With Another 'Liberal' on High Court." *U.S. News & World Report*, Sept. 11, 1967, p. 21.

"With Mr. Marshall on the Supreme Court." *U.S. News & World Report*, June 26, 1967, pp. 12–13.

"The World's Biggest Law Firm." *Ebony*, September 1953, pp. 17–22.

Other Sources

"Brown v. Board of Education of Topeka." *U.S. Supreme Court Report*, lawyer's edition, October 1953 Term, pp. 874–83.

"Thurgood Marshall." *Bulletin of Bibliography*, vol. 42, no. 2, June 1985.

"Thurgood Marshall: The Man." WNET-TV, New York, Sept. 22, 1988.

Index

162 | Index